Harold H. Weissman

OVERCOMING MISMANAGEMENT IN THE HUMAN SERVICE PROFESSIONS

Jossey-Bass Publishers

San Francisco · Washington · London · 1973

OVERCOMING MISMANAGEMENT IN THE HUMAN SERVICE PROFESSIONS
A Casebook of Staff Initiatives
by Harold H. Weissman

Copyright © 1973 by: Jossey-Bass, Inc., Publishers
615 Montgomery Street
San Francisco, California 94111
&
Jossey-Bass Limited
3 Henrietta Street
London WC2E 8LU

Library of Congress Catalogue Card Number LC 73-10944

International Standard Book Number ISBN 0-87589-212-4

Manufactured in the United States of America

JACKET DESIGN BY WILLI BAUM

FIRST EDITION

Code 7342

The Jossey-Bass
Behavioral Science Series

Preface

To my father,
Morris Weissman (1903–1971),
my first supervisor

A very unhappy social worker, after receiving a poor evaluation from a supervisor, once wrote: "Social welfare like all Gaul is divided into three parts. The first has until recently been inhabited by the Hierarchae, which may account for the fact that the field has been subject to unsteadiness. The second by the Supervisii, which explains why too many of the most able no longer work with those in need of help. They are in conference. And the last by the Reformae, who believe the populace is anxious to substitute social change for sex."

Had he been more dispassionate, this social worker might have pointed out that social welfare is also inhabited by thousands of hard-working, dedicated people who spend their lives under adverse situations with some of the most unhappy and unlucky people in the world and still manage to do a lot more good than bad. I have met many of these people in the course of writing this book, the purpose of which is to help staff in the service professions deal with problems in their organizations related to poor and ineffective management.

The problems of professionals in bureaucracies are not restricted to social work. These problems occur in any organization staffed by personnel who spend a considerable number of years developing a particular expertise. Professionals share a desire for and expect a large degree of autonomy from organizational control; they want maximum discretion in carrying out their professional activities, free from organizational interference or confining procedures. In addition, professionals tend to look to other professionals to gain some measure of self-esteem, are not likely to be devoted to any one organization, and accept a value system that puts great emphasis on the client's interest.

The bureaucrat is different from the professional. He performs specialized and routine activities under the supervision of a hierarchy of officials. His loyalty and career are tied up with his organization. Therefore, conflict results when professionals are asked to perform like bureaucrats.

During the 1960s, the bureaucratic problems of social agencies—confused procedures, unresponsiveness to clients, and ritualized regulations—occupied the attention of many social work professionals, especially those at the lower organizational levels. These lower level professionals were often the first to urge organizational change, and it is to them and their counterparts in teaching, nursing, and rehabilitation counseling that *Overcoming Mismanagement in the Human Service Professions* is primarily addressed.

It is important to focus on administrative problems from the point of view of what lower level staff can do about them without necessarily going through channels. Having the least authority, the line social worker feels the pinch of bureaucratic ineptness most severely. While a great deal has been written to help administrators do their job, little has been written to help the administered. When they are the victims of red tape, poor supervisors, archaic procedures, lack of teamwork, and confused priorities, the administered must either hope their administrators have read their own books, grin and bear it, or move on.

In order to provide social workers with other alternatives,

several analytic steps are followed in *Overcoming Mismanagement in the Human Service Professions*. First, review the tactics of organizational change developed in the 1960s ranging from client advocacy to participative management. Much can be learned from the successes and failures of this decade.

Second, little in present literature helps social workers anticipate the reactions of recalcitrant and inaccessible administrators. This knowledge is generally gained through bitter experience. Each of the case studies presented here describes tactics used by administrators to block change. Finally, workers are provided a set of countertactics to deal with expected resistance.

Considerable emphasis is given to describing how different social agencies function. Each of the chapters, other than the Prologue and the final chapter, utilizes a social agency setting as the focus of analysis. (The agency names are fictional; they represent composites of many different agencies. Any resemblance to actual social workers or other professionals is coincidental.) In essence, each of the chapters describes a part of a model of a social agency. The concluding chapter synthesizes the description of the model. As such, *Overcoming Mismanagement in the Human Service Professions* should also be of value to those whose job it is to administer and plan service programs.

Each chapter also focuses on a different set of complaints, not necessarily because they are endemic to that particular type of agency, but merely for illustrative purposes. The discussion is general enough so that the reader may extrapolate the problems and solutions to other settings.

Because there are many different ways to approach particular problems, the discussion about any one problem, such as an overburdened caseload, is not exhaustive. Rather, situations illustrate particular skills and techniques that workers can use in various situations. Thus, *Overcoming Mismanagement in the Human Service Professions* is best viewed as a handbook or compendium of ways in which lower level professional staff can initiate organizational change.

To achieve this end, I have written most of the book in an anecdotal case study style, to present the reader with the rich interplay of personal and structural elements in organizational life. (A social psychology of organizations is much needed, and the case study approach should help in its development.)

One other stylistic device bears mention. It is in my nature to use humor; and it is my judgment that both the inducers and the objects of change require large doses of humility if the boundaries of rational behavior in organizations are to be expanded. A modest humor can be of assistance.

All or most social agencies, administrators, and supervisors do not resemble those described here, although the caricatures presented may make this seem to be the case. The distortion is necessary because *Overcoming Mismanagement in the Human Service Professions* is for social workers who are not fortunate enough to work for able people or agencies. I have taken considerable pains to present clearly the severe pressures under which many administrators must work, and I believe that the level of analysis is beyond the simple "we the good" versus "they the bad."

Without the help of several hundred social workers who took the time to fill out a questionnaire and be interviewed, this book could not have been completed. I hope that the results are some small recompense. William Stafford, director of the New York Community Training Institute; Bertram Beck, then director of Mobilization for Youth; and Ruth Weintraub, now retired dean of social sciences, Hunter College, provided funds for clerical and research assistance. I am deeply appreciative. My colleagues Aaron Rosenblatt, Elaine Marshack, Bertram Beck, and Jessica Getzel read drafts of the text and provided valuable advice. Tom Ruben and Diane Craig, students of mine, were useful critics. Elaine Fox made the typing and proofreading a pleasure.

I pay tribute to others in the book. Most importantly, I thank all those colleagues over the years who have complained and to whom I have complained about the problems in the agencies in which we worked. I should especially like to thank Nancy Dorn, whose complaint was the one that made me begin to think that the problems of social agency administration were too important to be left entirely to either the administrators or the staff.

New York City   HAROLD H. WEISSMAN
September 1973

Contents

Overcoming Mismanagement
in the
Human Service Professions

A Casebook
of Staff Initiatives

 Prologue

Overcoming Mismanagement

Problems in bureaucracy are endless. They range from ritualism and overconformity to self-perpetuation and self-interest. Following the rules often becomes more important than achieving the goals, and organizations are run for the benefit of staff and administration rather than for clients.

Dumont (1970, pp. 10–12) puts it this way: "It is the unwritten rules, tacit but ever present, subtle but overwhelming, inarticulated but commanding, that determine the behavior of the men and women who buzz out their lives in the spaces defined by the [bureaucracy]. . . . These rules are few in number. Rule number 1 is to maintain your tenure. . . . The second rule of behavior . . . is to keep the boss from getting embarrassed. The third is to make sure that all appropriated funds are spent by the end of the fiscal year. . . . The fourth, keep the agency alive. . . .

1

The fifth and final unwritten rule . . . is to maintain a stable and well-circumscribed constituency."

As might be anticipated, workers develop a number of adaptations to these frustrating situations. In a purely bureaucratic adaptation, supervisors place the blame for workers' complaints on top management. The supervisor assures the worker that he is entitled to his own feelings but he must follow policy. Workers are subtly admonished that constant challenging of authority indicates a personality problem; a mature professional knows how to work within agency limits and agency policy.

In a professional adaptation, supervisors claim consistency between agency policies and professional norms even though they appear to be contradictory. The cold atmosphere in the waiting rooms is defended on the thesis that a little anxiety is good for treatment, and denial of welfare payments because relatives refuse to contribute is said to promote family stability.

In the professional approach, there is no appeal to self-discipline and conformity. Rather, an attempt is made to show that policies are fundamentally consistent with social work ideals and the interests of clients. This constantly defensive posture denies the existence of conflict and is extremely infuriating to line workers (Scott, 1969, pp. 120–121).

In a political adaptation, the rules and regulations are bent with the supervisor looking the other way while the worker does what he thinks should be done. Generally there is collusion between the worker and the supervisor: "If you do this, I won't bother you about that." The conspiratorial atmosphere created by collusion leaves the worker vulnerable and therefore afraid to confront the problems directly.

Most workers are unhappy with these adaptations. After a period of learning the job, many workers try to improve their own and the agency's functioning. Some give up quickly. Others accommodate, waiting for promotion to the higher ranks. A few continue the struggle, only to leave for other jobs when dissatisfaction mounts beyond their level of tolerance.

Nevertheless, during the 1960s many professionals at the lower levels of social agencies were deeply involved in urging institutional reform. Their prescriptions for change took several forms other than the above adaptations (Taebel, 1972).

Client advocacy was developed. The clients' interests were to be pursued at all costs. Each worker was to be an ombudsman, even at the risk of personal or agency conflict. Another tactic was the organization of clients to bring political pressure on the bureaucracies; sit-ins, confrontations, boycotts, and marches were the order of the day.

In a third approach, workers attempted to decentralize the bureaucracies and give the community control. This meant hiring local people to fill significant positions or seeking them out as volunteers to serve on policy-making boards. A fourth approach called for participative management. Hierarchies were to be flattened, lower level staff were to be included in decision-making, and democracy was to extend to the workplace.

While none of these was a panacea—local people often were as rigid and unsympathetic as nonlocals, few workers were willing to risk their jobs for clients, bureaucracies had more ways of fending off political pressure than were dreamt of, and democracies needed leaders, staff participation notwithstanding—they were all of some value in certain situations.

I contend that the failure of staff to bring about desired organizational changes in the 1960s was related to an inadequate conceptualization of a nonprofit organization. There is a crucial difference between the way profit-making and nonprofit-making organizations operate. Money serves as an alarm system in private enterprise: Ford sooner or later must respond to the tension caused by lack of Edsel sales.

Social Edsels do not produce the same tension in nonprofit organizations. Because the connection between the product produced and revenues received is indirect, social Edsels can go on for decades in the same ineffective way. There is no alarm system. Clients are seldom a source of pressure because they have few alternatives to the service. When the money-giving public is willing to let professionals decide what should be done, professionals often disagree privately since it is difficult to determine program success or failure. As money is almost always in short supply, administrators are loath to tie its receipt to ill-defined standards of success or failure. They prefer to be judged by the effort expended.

If Ford were funded on the basis of how hard people worked on the development of the Edsel, we would probably still have Edsels. It is of prime importance, therefore, to build an alarm system, similar to that provided by money for profit-making organizations, into nonprofit organizations.

Alarms galvanize organizational members into action because consequences become apparent. These consequences, both desired and undesired, comprise an essential part of an accountability system (the structure and procedures through which an organization gives an accounting of its activities). In many social agencies this system is severely flawed. For example: if boards of directors are to hold social agencies accountable, what will create the tension to push a board to insist on change? Keeping the board dependent on the administration for information about agency functioning dissipates tension rather than focuses it. The board is likely to get only the information that the administration wants it to get. What, then, are the consequences for poor management?

In the chapters that follow, considerable emphasis is placed on the means of rectifying such situations; for without an effective accountability system social agencies probably cannot solve their problems. And as a corollary, without an accountability system administration has little necessity to seriously consider the views and ideas of lower level staff. Nothing will happen to them if they don't.

The focus on consequences and accountability is also an important corrective to an overemphasis on rational humanism as a key to organizational change. Many lower level staff interviewed during the course of this study held the view that rationality, personal commitment on their part, open communication, and the inculcation of client-centered values were the levers of organizational change. They believed in the following change model: worker states a position or policy at staff meeting, executive appoints a committee to study the problem, committee reports back to staff, modifications are suggested, vote of approval is taken, and policy is implemented. Time span, hopefully, is one week.

At times such a model may work, probably where the proposed change involves no major redistribution of organization power or resources (Patti and Resnick, 1972). More often, disappointment and disillusionment are the result.

Most workers interviewed felt that if they were the executive director or the supervisor in their agency, they could do better than the incumbent. Perhaps so, but they were unable to be the director or the supervisor for that particular moment or situation about which they spoke. Their only hope was to take actions to ensure that their superiors carried out their jobs differently than they were presently doing.

To achieve such ends, rational persuasion is of limited usefulness. First, there is often a lack of verified knowledge in the field on how to deal with many social problems. How does one reform a juvenile delinquent, help an addict break his habit, cure a schizophrenic, patch up a broken home, or get a family off the relief rolls? These and other problems that social workers deal with are extremely complex and difficult. The lack of definitive knowledge introduces a range of judgment and discretion in social agency functioning with attendant disagreement.

Second, the personal desires or ends of all levels of staff are not necessarily congruent with organizational ends. Some workers want promotions, some security, some innovation, and some simply rest. They will not easily be persuaded to give up or postpone the fulfillment of their desires for a change of seemingly dubious merit.

Third, certain conflicts in program goals such as between custody and treatment or stability and innovation affect members of a social agency differently. The resolution of such strains through rational planning and decision-making is constrained by rather strong limits on the cognitive capacity of key staff members, the internal goal consistency of complex organizations, and the speed with which the organization can gather facts.

> Quasiresolution of Conflict. *The goal preferences of various participants are mutually inconsistent in the sense that not every participant's most preferred alternative can be achieved. Organizations therefore do not have a simple rank order of goals but exist with conflicts of interest which are resolved either through compromise or sequential attention to goals.*

Uncertainty Avoidance. *Organizations abhor uncertainty. They tend to avoid it rather than deal with it. They
emphasize short-run problems and attempt to control the environment rather than predict it. If "good . . . practice" is stand-
ardized (through professional associations, journals, word of
mouth, external consultants), one can be reasonably confident.
The environment becomes manageable.*

Problemistic Search. *Search for solutions to organizational problems is simple minded. It is dictated by the existence
of problems rather than the desire to understand the workings of
the system. It proceeds on the basis of a simple model of causal-
ity until driven to a more complex one by failure.*

Organizational Learning. *When an organization discovers a solution to a problem by searching in a particular way,
it will be more likely to search in that way on future problems
of the same type. Likewise with failure [Cyert and March, 1964,
pp. 291–298].*

Thus, most decisions tend to be based on a variety of factors:
what the known facts are and how they are interpreted; the power
and prestige that proponents can bring to bear; the potential rewards, jobs, promotions, and status that will become available; and,
ultimately, the effect of the decisions on the survival of the agency.
Rational persuasion about the value of particular programs or procedures to clients seldom carries the day.

While administration has the formal authority to make
decisions and see that they are implemented, it depends on its
ability to secure consent for these decisions. Firing is costly and
time-consuming. For professional staff who disagree with decisions,
opportunities to drag their feet, interpret rules ritualistically, or
scapegoat clients are plentiful. Authority is necessary but not sufficient for running an organization.

Influence based on sources other than formal authority is
required. Influence is the ability to get others to act, think, or feel
as one intends. As Banfield notes (1961, p. 4), influence may rest
upon a sense of obligation or respect for authority or on improvement in the logic or information available (rational persuasion). It
may also rest upon a desire to gratify the influencer (friendship,
benevolence); on changing the influencee's perception of the

behavior alternatives open to him or his evaluation of them (through selling, suggestion, fraud, or deception rather than by rational persuasion); or on inducing him to select as his preferred (or least objectionable) alternative the one chosen for him by the influencer through rewards and punishments. Administration utilizes all these sources of influence. While these are analytical distinctions, they are crucial in terms of this book as it takes up at the point where administration is not open to change solely through discussion or persuasion.

If social workers are to do anything about problems of salary, working conditions, supervisor competence, lack of teamwork, lack of accessibility of administration, and lack of success with clients, they require a range of influence similar to that possessed by administration.

A line worker begins with only his intelligence, the authority of his office, and his own personality as his sources of influence in the agency. How he can pyramid these resources into additional sources of influence and how he can bring this influence to bear in organizations are the main themes of this book.

In the chapters that follow, the specific ways staff can pursue these ends are analyzed. Information, people, and instruments are key building blocks of influence. A range of techniques and mechanisms for gaining access to these sources of influence is explored—from simply developing a reputation for competence, to organizing unions, to mounting public exposés in the media.

Nevertheless, an increase in lower participant influence does not necessarily lead to desired changes. Where this influence can be brought to bear and how the organization will react to it must also be considered. As noted, in the 1960s bureaucracies were generally able to ward off influence (usually based on threats) posed by clients and staff.

Influence is best viewed as a dynamic process. When influence is exerted, a price must be paid. How much is it worth to X to get Y to act in a certain fashion? How many promotions can be made, how many people can be fired?

At some point the disadvantages of using a particular type of influence outweigh the advantages. Many people, both administrators and staff, who have sufficient influence to take certain actions choose not to because of the price to be paid. This reluctance by administrators can become an important lever for staff in devising ways of pyramiding their influence over organizational decisions and procedures.

Who has the power to make certain decisions and what it takes to influence them in a particular direction are obviously important questions. Therefore, each of the cases in this book is presented in terms of a description of the problem and the attempts of staff to deal with it; an analysis of how these attempts usually fail because of the counterinfluences administration can bring to bear; and the means and the attendant price staff have to pay to develop the requisite influence to achieve their ends.

One aspect of this price deserves specific mention. Keeping nonprofit organizations from going bad is a difficult job. Those who seek to change organizations should be clear about their motives. One certainty is that change usually meets resistance and that this resistance seldom is gentle. Conflict itself is seldom as pleasant in reality as it is in contemplation. Not all change need result in conflict or even great disagreement, but they had best be prepared.

Another reason for knowing one's motives is quite simply that all change is not for the good. The ability to ascertain and be critical of one's proposals is probably the major requirement for effectiveness in organizational life.

The difficulty with scrutinizing one's own motivation as well as that of others is that there is seldom a single motive that impels one to action. Rewards, other than altruism and a desire to help, motivate most social workers. Rather than deny the legitimacy of such desires and strivings, one should use them as the starting point for analysis. For example, one can be both hostile and correct in one's appraisals. Likewise, administrators can be nasty people and still make the right decisions.

Too often those who criticize and wish to change agencies revert in anger and frustration to the same old psychological explanations of organizational problems. "The supervisor hates men." A balance is required between psychological and social analysis. There is little point in diagnosing problems in ways which, even if they are accurate, are not particularly useful for the solution of the problems. To do so is merely good description. What follows is meant to be operational.

1

Promoting
Teamwork

For those who wish to change organizations, knowledge of how organizations function is crucial. Each of the case studies presented is geared to adding to this knowledge. This first chapter looks at the central role leadership and peer relationships play in agency life. It also introduces a major dynamic of organizations: their reward system. What organizational actors want from their job is not necessarily the same as what their organizations offer them. To gain acceptance of new programs and policies one must know the priorities of those who must live with these programs and policies.

Organizations offer their participants utilitarian rewards such as money and promotions; emotional rewards such as friendship, status, and a sense of competence; and ideological rewards such as being a good social worker or fulfilling one's political commitments. There are also rewards which accrue to departments and to the organization as a whole such as funds, prestige, and security.

Since there are seldom enough rewards to go around, there is often conflict.

In fact, the most exciting modern day feuds no longer take place in the Appalachian mountains. Many of them are fought out in social agencies. Lower level staff had best be prepared as the feuds are often couched in terms of improving service to the clients. The Hatfields and the McCoys would know better.

Feuds such as those between psychologists and psychiatrists are based on long standing rivalries outside of any one particular organization. Others are over allocations of space, facilities, and money inside the organization. Some are related to the authority structure in an organization: who can tell whom what to do, or who should be able to; and who gets more money than whom, and for what.

In every organization, there are informal organizations that can either call off or intensify the feuds. These informal organizations develop as staff interact with one another for mutual assistance in getting the job done, for communication about factors in the agency which affect their work, for mutual protection and job security, and for a sense of justice and equity about the quantity and quality of work they do.

Likewise, in every organization, there are informal leaders. These leaders can often be discovered by watching the patterns of people who eat together, take coffee breaks together, or give assistance to one another (Blau, 1955).

This informal system provides the staff with interpretations of a variety of facets of agency life. For example, if the administration wants to create a certain change, the informal organization can give it a coloration: "they simply want to make us work harder," or "it's a very good idea." The informal organization translates organizational actions into personal rewards and costs. Yet the informal system is by no means always cohesive. There may in fact be cliques and considerable conflict.

Scope of the Problem

For years Western State Psychiatric Institute has been a battleground for professional Hatfields and McCoys. Many of the buildings in this hospital date from the nineteenth century, and it is the oldest psychiatric facility in the Midwest. From a distance it looks like an old college campus: broad sidewalks connect the buildings and the lush grounds give the feeling that this is a pleasant place. The shock occurs upon entering the buildings. The ceilings are high and the corridors have that empty hollow ring. There is no happiness here.

Western State is one of five state hospitals in a large midwestern state. It covers an area including the largest city in the state and an adjacent county. Recently the hospital has undergone a major administrative change. It is unitized. Each of the seven main buildings operates as a separate hospital and receives its patients only from specified geographical areas. Each hospital is supposed to work closely with the community that it serves. At present, this community relationship has yet to develop.

Each of the seven hospitals has its own director who is responsible to an executive director for the whole complex. Western State receives its funds mainly from the state, although in the past it has received federal funds for research studies being carried on by staff psychiatrists at the hospital. Patients seldom pay anything.

The hospital has a reputation for being the worst of the five state hospitals in relation to the use of new and innovative treatment techniques, general atmosphere, and patient care. The situation is related to its proximity to a large city. Pressure on the hospital to change has been less intense simply because the metropolitan area contains a progressive city hospital and several private mental hospitals, most of which are affiliated with universities.

Carol Whitebone became interested in mental illness during her master's training at the University of Chicago. She purposely chose to work in a state mental hospital after receiving her M.S.W. She had no illusions about conditions but felt a commitment to work with those who needed her skills most.

She is small, with light blond hair. Her main strength is that she knows what she wants. This is always a surprise to residents and other staff members, for to look at Carol one would think that the slightest breeze would blow her over. Her other main quality is intelligence. She knows, for example, that because she looks so unassuming and speaks softly, people seldom feel threatened by her. She can say many things that others cannot.

Carol works in unit two, which receives most of its patients from the south side of the nearby metropolis, an area comprising well over half a million people. There are seven wards in unit two. The first five are open and patients may walk in and out and around the grounds. Wards six and seven are locked, and they contain patients who are potentially violent or unable to care for their normal functioning.

Carol works on ward five. Each of the open wards has the same staff picture—a resident in charge, five nurses, a social worker, two case aides, and four attendants. Ward five has an A and B corridor and a patient capacity of one hundred which is almost always filled.

Dr. Connors directs unit two and was an ardent advocate of electroshock therapy when he first came to the hospital in the early 1950s. Over the years, he has found himself in increasing conflict with a succession of executive directors who were oriented to various interpersonally directed therapies. The current director's main concern is milieu therapy.

There is a great deal of gossip about Connors. He is rumored to be an alcoholic. Most of the staff view him as an obstructionist to any new idea. Connors is seldom seen on the wards and is known to have some connection with a private sanatorium in a small town twenty miles to the northwest.

Some of the problems at Western State are related to the staff psychiatrists. Many cannot sustain a private practice or show enough competence to get higher status jobs; and the residents in psychiatry are generally the least able students. A great number of residents are foreign students from non-English-speaking countries who have come to America for training in psychiatry. Some of these residents have a language problem, thus compounding the difficulties of the job.

The word in the hospital is that doctors are never fired. In fact, doctors are seldom fired as it is very difficult to replace them. There are constant rumors about the psychopathology of various doctors. One or two have in fact had psychotic episodes.

Most patients at Western State have been on a well-traveled

route. They or their family have insufficient money to place them in a private hospital. Therefore, they are hospitalized in the city's main psychiatric hospital, North Shore General. If their condition indicates that they cannot be discharged within a few weeks, they are sent from North Shore to Western State. Because of the crowded situation at Western State, every attempt is made to return patients to the community. A high percentage of such returned patients are then readmitted to North Shore, then to Western State, and so on. Often, if a patient has been on the route several times, he will remain permanently at Western State in a forgotten ward. Patients who are admitted for the first time get better treatment.

Organizations, like religions, have a faith. This faith is simply the feeling that what the organization is doing and the ways in which it is doing it are worthwhile and helpful for both individuals and society as a whole. To paraphrase Jay (1969, pp. 204–205), some agencies are extremely religious. They hold regular revival (staff) meetings at which rousing hymns are sung to the glory of the agency and its achievements. Staff are encouraged to stand up and give passionate personal testimony. There is a trenchant sermon from the executive and a hate session for flailing the devils of poor public understanding and harmful practices of competitors.

If an agency built its reputation and success on the assumption that people really want meaningful long-term relationships with their therapists, then a group asserting the contrary—people really want the help of drugs and speedy return to the community— would undermine all the expertness, all the practices, all the staff training, and all the client loyalty and public support the agency has built up over the years. In agency religions as in others, the heretic must be cast out, not because he is probably wrong, but because he might be right.

At stake in organizational feuds are not only reputations and skills on both sides, but the idea that one side is useless to the organization. Of course, the argument is couched on what is good for the client, but it turns out that what is good for the client is also good for the person arguing for the client.

Line workers are often shocked to hear that their suggestions are interpreted by their superiors as simply a desire to take over the superior's job. This is generally not in the line worker's mind. Yet, if suggestions are accepted and taken to their organizational conclusion, such indeed may become the fact.

A mortal struggle is beginning to build up at Western State. The implications were first noted in the struggle over unitization and are becoming clearer as the attempt is made to relate the hospital closer to the community. Utilizing the community as a treatment resource and returning the patient to the community as quickly as possible could put into question the skills of those who have advanced insight therapy as the major treatment modality.

The conflict over organizational methods had direct ramifications on the working conditions at Western State. No one seemed to be in charge. When Carol came in 1965, there was no private office where she could interview clients. She had to share a telephone with everyone on the staff, and it was almost impossible to get typing done when it was needed. To get a piece of paper or a pencil she had to resort to scheming. According to one staff member, "There is nothing you want to get done that you can get done honestly here." Procedures and lines of authority were simply too confused.

The top administration simply did not communicate with the staff. They were afraid that the staff would be able to make demands if it got any information. It was similar to the dictator's fear of what the people will do if they find out what is happening.

On the other hand, administration often acted as if it had no authority at all. When asked about relating the hospital more closely to the community, administration responded that the state commission of mental health was not ready. When Carol tactfully queried the chief of social service, the response was, "The administration is always fighting cutbacks in the budget. It has to fight very hard to stand still."

The real complexity of changing hospital policy became apparent to Carol during the attempt to institute milieu therapy as a prelude to the community approach. Milieu therapy involves an orientation in which each staff person, psychiatrist, social worker, nurse, aide, and attendant, plus the hospital rules, structure, and climate are considered to have an impact on patients. Staff meet together periodically as a team to discuss progress of patients and to plan and coordinate various procedures and activities. An attempt is also made to organize committees of patients to plan for ward procedure and to help develop the therapeutic milieu (Rossi and Filstead, 1972).

The reality of the team was something quite different than anticipated. The degree of staff retraining that the team approach would require was underestimated. There is nothing in the training of resident psychiatrists to equip them to lead a team of staff. They know very little about the normal group processes of people at work, have little insight into the role of authority in nontherapeutic relationships, and have little knowledge of how the social structure of the ward affects the individual psyche.

On many wards there were nurses who had worked at Western State for twenty to thirty years. Their whole method of operation simply could not be changed overnight (Wertz, 1966). Perhaps the greatest miscalculation was the effect of the change to milieu therapy on the attendants. Since the attendants spent a great deal of time with the patients, hopefully they could be of great use therapeutically. While this idea has good potential, attendants require more retraining than anyone. Many attendants held the opinion that patients were at Western State because they had done bad things, should have been in prison, and were lucky to be at Western State.

To counter this, classes were set up for the attendants. It turned out that the attendants were more off the wards taking classes than on the wards taking care of patients. Those attendants who were sympathetic to patients prior to the shift responded well to the team approach; those that were not sympathetic were not much affected.

Another social worker told Carol, "If I sit down with an attendant to talk to him about patient discharge, he says, 'I'm not paid for this.' I understand his feeling because the attendants are most subject to the whims of the administration. Some took the job just to be cleaning people. Any other demand is something they just don't want. Many are holding two jobs because the pay is so low. They see the residents goofing off. The doctors have private practices and are hardly ever here. Everyone playing an angle makes them feel that the whole system is a fraud. They play their own angles too.

"For example, on many of the wards the patients work for the attendants rather than vice versa. Some patients clean out the bathrooms, others help with the distribution of the food. The attendants kick up a fuss when certain patients are to be discharged, therapeutic team or no therapeutic team. They need them to help. Added to all this is the terrific pressure of the numbers of patients. The hospital is a dumping ground. And then there is the turnover of staff. It's a little bit like a revolving door in a busy department store at lunch time."

When a patient government council was set up, the situation became even more confused. Patients began making rules which affected the attendants' work procedures. The attendants refused covertly to carry out the council's decisions. Dominated by the more vocal patients, the council was realistically concerned about patients' needs, but had little understanding or feeling for attendants' needs and desires.

Another major problem with the theory of the therapeutic team soon became obvious to Carol. The theory does not explain what is to be done with staff who either refuse or are unable to change their old methods. Civil service and unions make it difficult to fire, and wages are often so low that replacements cannot easily be found.

Resistance to Change

Shortly after coming to the hospital in 1965, Carol joined an informal group of staff who were terribly concerned about conditions on the forgotten wards. Since she was new at the hospital, Carol did not play a major role in this affair. The staff began systematically documenting the situation on the forgotten wards. They brought their reports to the chief of social services and ultimately to the attention of the director of the hospital. There were a variety of delays, half promises, and training programs set up without very much result. Finally, a worker who had already secured a job in another state decided to feed the information to a newspaper reporter he knew. The papers had a field day with the situation, complete with gruesome pictures. The exposé reached the state commission and a full-blown investigation took place, covered extensively by the media.

As a result, in 1967 the Western State Asylum became the Western State Psychiatric Institute. A new director was hired whose main concern was milieu therapy. There was considerable elation among members of Carol's group. Yet, in 1972, the situation in the forgotten wards had not really changed. Only physical brutality was now more of an isolated phenomenon. The exposé had left intact the basic situation which caused the problems: confused goals, conflicting authority systems, overwhelming numbers of patients, and most important, no effective accountability system. The exposé might have been effective if those who organized it had developed a plan for change that was rooted in the reality of the hospital.

The therapeutic milieu was not an operationalized plan for change. It was a goal. Short of an effective plan, they required an ongoing watchdog group to monitor the changes. They had neither.

For example, in situations where jobs are to be drastically changed, staff, as well as nature, abhors a vacuum. The vacuum game begins on a simple enough note. A worker wants to decide where and when he shall work, control the resources for his work, and have some security that his job will be there the next day.

In so doing, each worker finds ultimately that he must expand his jurisdiction. He quickly discovers that to control his own job, he must poach on the authority and preserves given to other people's jobs. Generally, these other people are his superiors. All too frequently, superiors find certain aspects of their job onerous. They tend to emphasize the aspects they like and create a vacuum elsewhere. Many doctors simply wish to dispense medicine, see patients on a one-to-one basis, and then attend to their private affairs. Carol's resident did not like the team meetings and the confrontations and arguments that occurred at them. Gradually, he turned the leadership of the meetings over to Carol.

Carol's team worked fairly well compared to the other teams in the unit. She had informal relationships with many of the staff persons, yet even she met resistances. Intellectually the social workers had the capacity to run the teams. But they didn't have the capacity to confer rewards—promotions, changes in working hours —to the other staff.

Her friends on the other wards had considerably more difficulty. The nurses had resisted what they considered the illegitimate assumption of authority by the social workers. They had already forgotten more about mental illness than the social workers would ever know. These staff members rigidly defined the boundaries of their jobs with "I am not paid to do that." As Jay (1969, p. 32) notes, this attitude is surprisingly akin to that of the male hippopotamus, who indicates to other hippopotami the extent of his turf by defecating around its perimeter. Outside his circle others can do what they want, but if they come within it, they're in for a fight.

Strategy

Most social workers tend to quit places like Western State after a year or two. It is difficult to quarrel with their decision. Carol chose to stick it out; the hospital was lucky she did, for Carol saved the therapeutic milieu.

There is nothing so frustrating as having a good idea and finding it lost in the organizational maze. The line social worker has to sell his idea to a supervisor who sells it to his supervisor, who sells it to the administration, who sells it to someone else to provide the funds. Most people and most ideas simply fold up in such a context. The selling of an idea, as Carol learned, is a skill that can be developed.

She recognized that it is generally easier to tell when a particular therapy does not work than when it does. The field of mental health has never really developed adequate indices of success. What is success with a paranoid schizophrenic? Maintaining him in the community, enabling him to wash and clothe himself, or returning him to so-called normal functioning with his family and friends?

Western State, overwhelmed with the crushing numbers of mental patients, never has had time to really take stock of what it would consider success. Thus, there is a constraint on the part of many to try whatever is new—behavior therapy, lobotomies, recreational therapy, milieu therapy, short-term hospitalization, and work therapy. To a certain extent new ideas are required to keep up the morale of the staff and the institution. The field is ripe for fads.

After a few years at Western State, Carol developed a healthy skepticism; but developing a therapeutic milieu did seem a reasonable approach to take. Yet, it quickly became clear that as the whole hospital suddenly shifted toward this orientation, more was being lost than gained. The scope and substance of the proposed changes were of such broad dimensions that overwhelming resistance was occurring.

A Do-Good Organizational Secret: Significant plans generally find significant opponents who, if they cannot stymie a plan in one fashion, will try another. They do not give up simply because they have been outvoted.

Considering the hospital's problems, some staging of the project was necessary if the attempt to institute milieu therapy was to be salvaged. To achieve this, Carol used a tactic which she had developed over the years: the more directors or supervisors believe an idea is their own, the more likely they are to act on it.

There was already an ongoing committee to advise on program. This committee, composed solely of chiefs of services, could never come to any conclusions. There were two major flaws in the committee: it had no direct input from lower levels of staff and the executive director of the hospital had stopped attending the meetings.

Unless the executive director was present throughout the discussions, it would be difficult to influence him or secure any action. Carol and her supervisor got the executive director, who was aware of some of the problems with the program, to agree to attend and expand the composition of the group.

From the committee meetings it became clear to everyone that staff was confused about what was expected of them. When expectations were clarified, many staff did not have the requisite skills. Material and equipment were often not available. And most important, administrators were unaware of the changes in existing organizational arrangements (intake policy, salary schedules, discharge criteria) that would be required if milieu therapy were instituted.

The executive director had blithely assumed that he could delegate responsibility for implementation. Knowing what and when to delegate is a crucial function of leadership. He had not recognized the need for ongoing feedback of information to pick up problems and resolve them. Nor had he understood the difficulties the staff would encounter in trying to conform to the new role expectations.

Once the complexity of the situation became apparent, the idea of staging the project became obvious. Carol never had to make the suggestion. The executive director chose a unit whose director was interested in milieu therapy. Personnel desiring to work on the project would be transferred. As they became trained, they would be retransferred to other units. The units would thus be converted slowly, one ward at a time. Problems and unanticipated consequences could be negotiated with a minimum of confusion or potential harm.

Carol was particularly adroit at this later stage of discussion. She recognized that while training, feedback and sharing of authority and responsibility were vital to a team's operation, some jobs are more taxing and stressful, some have strict time demands, some are underpaid. For there to be effective shared decision-making, the strains must also be shared. For example, if the attendants are to be part of the team, then social workers and other staff should feel the strain attendants are under.

Carol suggested that every social worker act as attendant one week during the year. This experience makes it more likely that shared decision-making will reflect clearer understanding of ramifications. One of her colleagues put it thusly: "Attendants don't expect social workers to bathe patients, but they expect that social workers will pitch in in an emergency." By doing so, social workers convey the importance of the attendants to the team as well as a sense of respect for their efforts.

One of the most frequent complaints of social workers concerns the working conditions that they must endure. Without private offices, how can they talk confidentially and intimately with patients? Without their own telephone, how can people reach them? Yet, providing a private room for social workers on a ward geared to the team approach and milieu therapy would create great conflicts with the nurses and attendants who have no such privacy.

Schemes for team approaches in mental hospitals or residential treatment homes often miss the effect on the status and prestige of the poorest paid employees—the guard, the attendant, the cottage parent. The lowest status person on the team is often the person that the patient or inmate sees as most important. This low status person derives a sense of importance from his ability to get respect from the patient or inmate. He gets this respect from his ability to withhold or grant certain rewards such as weekend passes or access to the commissary.

When whole new systems of interaction are introduced, what little power low status staff have is often taken away. This can lead to attempts to sabotage the program as a way of fighting for what little control they have (McCleery, 1961).

Discussion

There are three basic strategies of change (Brager, 1967, pp. 115–118). Demonstration strategies assume that a proposed change can be demonstrated definitively and proved effective. Knowledge and research are the primary resources required. This strategy works best when the parties involved share a general consensus as to values and perspectives about what should be done. Such consensus is seldom easily maintained, if ever achieved.

In an integrative strategy, successful innovation rests on negotiating, bargaining, and involving all concerned in solving problems. This strategy assumes that good relationships and heightened communication will promote change. It also assumes that there is a shared commitment to a common value system, and differences occur only over priorities and tactics.

A pressure strategy assumes basic dissension between contending parties over values and priorities. This strategy implies that force must be applied and power brought to bear.

Often these strategies must be orchestrated because there is a difference between gaining agreement to change and actually implementing the change. Carol Whitebone was fortunate that top administration supported milieu therapy. Thus she was able to adopt an integrative strategy: educating, negotiating, and bargaining. subsequent chapters, are related to the *initiation* of change—getting the organization to change the behavior of its members and its procedures in a specified way. Many of her friends in other hospitals had program ideas that no one in their administration was interested in discussing. Their difficulties, as well as those of most workers in subsequent chapters, are related to the initiation of change—getting an organization to define a problem and decide on a way to resolve it (Gross, Giacquinta, Bernstein, 1971, p. 17).

With either set of difficulties, workers often will be required to possess the kind of personal forbearance that Carol demonstrated. Recognition as a brilliant worker or leader was not her concern. She encouraged others to take the lead when their positions were better suited to such activity. She was able to let others discover the solutions to the problems on the wards. Had Carol sought personal glory it is unlikely that she would have been able to move freely from leading the movement for change to following the lead of others as the process developed.

2

Selecting Program
Goals

The most common error that line workers make in trying to influence their agencies is to attempt organizing staff support before they understand the nature of the organizations in which they function. One main gap in this understanding is related to the different levels of rewards and costs in agencies. One can promote or demote an individual, enhance or tarnish the prestige of a department, or secure or jeopardize the survival of the agency. An action which may be rewarding in one sense may be very costly in others.

A second and equally damaging gap in understanding is the ignorance of how boards of directors operate. They do not function as a type of supreme court to adjudicate between staff and administration. Alfred Chasid, whose case follows, understood neither this fact nor the problems his actions caused at different organizational levels of the Cooperative Community Centers.

Scope of the Problem

The Cooperative Community Centers was started in the middle of the nineteenth century. Its basic goal is spreading the principles of Americanism among young men and women. It has constantly sought to interest youth in its ideals through a program of recreation and informal education. Programs have ranged from basketball and swimming to lecture series and concerts to neighborhood cleanup campaigns and other civic betterment projects. It is probably fair to say that there is not a program conceived of for young adults that the Cooperative Community Centers has not tried.

A branch of CCC exists in almost every city in America over ten or fifteen thousand population. In the large cities, there may be ten to twenty branch offices. Although there is a national board of directors, the local board in each city has almost complete control over the programs in its area. This board hires the director and gives approval to the various programs sponsored.

The funds for the CCC come from a number of sources: the community chest or united fund, membership dues, and private donations and contributions. In addition, the CCC is involved in governmental projects such as OEO job-training and day care.

The Lake City CCC includes fifteen branch offices, a central office, and a large residence. The executive director, a city-wide accounting and personnel service, and an assistant director for program who supervises the work of the branch directors are at the central office. In addition, there are a number of staff specialists in such areas as Americanism, physical education, and camping. The CCC also maintains a central public relations office.

Although the branch offices vary in size, in general each is headed by a director who has under him a variety of staff specialists, including a physical education director, a club director, and staff associates responsible for programs for various age groups. In larger branches, there are assistant directors to handle the financial matters.

For years, the CCC has maintained its own training school. It has never depended on schools of social work, and few of its staff have master's degrees. The core of its training is drawn from ideas about sound and healthy recreation rather than from group work rooted in progressive education and group dynamics. Nevertheless, the CCC's goals are the same as the goals of any settlement house or community center—the desire to produce healthy, adaptable people.

The Cooperative Community Center's board of directors in Lake City is comprised of businessmen and junior executives from many of the leading local corporations. Membership on the board is a mark of social standing and the men take their jobs seriously, especially the younger junior executives. The style of the CCC's administration mirrors that of a corporation. Accounting procedures are professional, a personnel committee of the board meets regularly, and authority is hierarchically organized.

The CCC's personnel have traditionally been Protestant and white. During the 1960s, the great shifts in population in the cities changed the neighborhoods in which the branches were located. To meet the challenge of minority neighborhoods, the CCC attempted to hire more black personnel, some with M.S.W. degrees. In addition, the increasing opportunity for employment in the social welfare field in the 1960s allowed staff to leave for better jobs, and the CCC has been forced to recruit from other than its own training schools. Increasingly some of the newer employees have M.S.W.s and are nonwhite or non-Protestant.

Over the years, the CCC developed into a family bureaucracy. The personnel could look forward to a life of employment in the agency as they moved from one city to another, shared common expectations and ideals, and developed knowledge of the ins and outs of agency procedures and policies. The dramatic symbol of their common identity was the informal expectation that each would contribute a percentage of his salary to the CCC movement.

The changes in the composition of the staff have had the unanticipated consequence of bringing conflict into the family. This situation was typified by the hiring of Alfred Chasid, a recently graduated M.S.W., to be the director of teenagers at a branch office in a Puerto Rican neighborhood. Chasid was trained in group work and community organization. Donating part of his salary to the CCC was not his idea of demonstrating commitment.

Centro Portoricenos Unidos, Chasid's center, was started

through funds provided by the Office of Economic Opportunity. Though these funds were for a one-year period, the central board of the CCC decided to continue the program on a provisional basis. The director of CPU had been an assistant director in one of the larger branches, had had a long career in the CCC, and had been trained by the CCC. The other staff members were mainly college graduates. One was a local Puerto Rican who had only a high school education.

Chasid was anxious that the center involve itself with the problems of housing, schools, and employment in the neighborhood. Given his rather small staff of five full-time workers, the center's director felt that more could be achieved by recreation and club programs as there was no other such resource in the whole community. He was also quite concerned about funding for the center as money had been given only provisionally for one year. The central board might simply cut off the funds. Therefore, he decided to move cautiously. Here, then, was the classic dispute over agency goals.

What should the goals be? It is not at all clear that the problems of housing and schools can be solved at the local level. Yet, while some people in the neighborhood desire recreation, others require more intensive and comprehensive kinds of services. Given limited resources, whichever decision is made, some will benefit and others will lose. Chasid was sophisticated and intelligent. Aware of the dilemma, he nevertheless decided to pursue his point of view.

Resistance to Change

Chasid began his campaign by speaking up at staff meetings. He made a variety of arguments centered around the word "relevance." In private conferences with the director, he constantly mentioned problems about the schools and employment. This tactic is best labeled rhetoric.

There are a variety of responses to rhetoric ranging from deafness to logical counterarguments. In this particular case, Chasid's director pointed out that he was already quite busy with the very extensive club and camping program. Nevertheless, he said that he would discuss potential new programs with the assistant director of the CCC at his next conference. This, of course, is the elementary countertactic of discussions at higher levels. Delay is then introduced.

The director sees the CCC assistant director once a month. At the time of the meeting, the assistant director is unexpectedly called out and the issue is not discussed. It will have to wait another month. The next conference comes, and Chasid is told that the assistant director would like to think it over.

Delay has a definite function. It tests resolve. An extremely high percentage of requests and ideas are dropped in this manner. If you do not drop it, how many times can you ask the boss the same question? It's embarrassing and ultimately anger producing.

For most people, this potential discomfort leads to procrastination and more delay; but Chasid was well versed in the "have you had your confrontation today" school of organizational change. After three months of badgering he got his answer. The assistant director talked it over with the director, and he thought that it would be a good idea to continue the present program. At the end of the year, a more objective appraisal could be made of the total program. Chasid's director got just the answer he wanted.

Chasid decided to escalate the battle by organizing the staff. While this tactic is a much-used one, it seldom works well. Chasid composed a petition to the assistant director to come and discuss the center's program. He had talked it over with staff members individually over lunch many times; yet, when he circulated the statement, several of the staff objected to the wording and said they could not sign. Others said they would not.

This was especially embarrassing to Chasid because two of the people who refused to sign were Puerto Rican women from the neighborhood who were on the clerical staff. He had thought it a wise tactic to have both service and clerical staff sign, especially since most of the clerical staff were local people. As he thought about the situation, he realized that one clerical worker was a widow with two children. She couldn't afford to antagonize the director. Another clerical worker intimated to him that he had a master's degree and could get a job any time he wanted it; she might have some trouble.

Later that afternoon came the administrative countertactic,

best termed "hoisted on your own petard." One of the secretaries had mentioned to the director that a petition about change in program was being circulated. He called Chasid into his office. He did not want to see the petition, but he could not understand why it was being done outside of the staff meeting in a secretive manner. After all, Chasid was always saying that decisions should be made out in the open, with full knowledge and full opportunity for participation.

Chasid stuttered that he fully intended to bring it to the staff meeting. It was, in fact, discussed at the next staff meeting, but with less impact than Chasid would have liked. When the director pointed out that a shift in program would mean dropping other programs, there was considerable hesitation. At the end of the discussion, the director nevertheless suggested that it might be a good idea if he invited the assistant director to come down and discuss the matter with the group.

The assistant director of CCC came on April 5. The meeting began with a brief talk by the assistant about the total program of the agency and concluded with his thanking the staff for all the effort that they had made and in particular for their interest in new programs. The discussion was somewhat of a rehash of the initial staff meeting, but the assistant's concluding remarks were on a hopeful note. He was going to bring their ideas to the board program committee for discussion. Chasid, of course, was very disheartened. After all, he was not a slow learner. By this time he could spot a delay. He considered quitting, but his friends convinced him that social change requires dedication and conviction.

Chasid returned to work on May 1 with a new resolve. He would not let the administration wear him down. The administration really had no intention of doing that. However, even though it was not planned by the administration, a new countertactic was transpiring as an unanticipated consequence of protracted negotiations—the EGO trap.

On May 15, the director of the center told Chasid that the CCC assistant director was tremendously enthusiastic about the meeting at the center and was particularly impressed with the way Chasid had explained his program ideas. Shortly thereafter, the assistant director asked Chasid to write a proposal for a job-training program. There was a deadline of June 30. Did he think he could make it? Of course, he could make it. As a matter of fact, he stayed up late several nights writing the proposal. The other staff actually contributed very little. Ego is running wild at this point.

Proposals have a way of taking a considerable amount of time to be finalized. Chasid's proposal was submitted on June 30. Finally, on September 15, OEO granted the center fifteen thousand dollars and Chasid was ecstatic. During the period from May to October, Chasid's criticism of the agency had toned down a bit. When the money arrived, he hoped to apply for the position of director of the job-training program as he was anxious to lock horns with some of the discriminatory unions in Lake City.

On November 15, the money arrived and the program officially started. A former Puerto Rican employee of the welfare department was hired for the job. Chasid could hardly complain; his Spanish was not particularly good, and he had consistently championed the hiring of blacks and Puerto Ricans. He did his best to make the new job-training counselor feel at home in the agency.

Unfortunately, by mid-January it was clear that the job-training counselor had a different idea of the program than Chasid. From the counselor's experience at welfare, he determined that the program could be maximally effective if it served only those who were motivated enough to make the best use of it. Chasid's plan had been to reach everyone, especially the most down and out.

Instead of urging the agency to plan for the implementation of the program prior to its initiation, his ego led him to assume that he would be allowed to do it himself. In February, Chasid met an old friend who knew of an opening at another agency. The director of this agency interviewed Chasid and told him about all of his plans for the future. On April 1 Chasid gave notice.

Strategy

It is difficult to find the villain in this situation. Certainly, the director might have been more concerned about the desires of the neighborhood. Nevertheless, since Chasid was the protagonist, he bears greatest criticism. Did he really think that a little rhetoric and five staff people could change a century-old agency?

A Do-Good Organizational Secret: Rather than reevaluate their goals, agencies prefer to reevaluate their workers. They occasionally alter this preference when their funds, legitimacy, or status is threatened.

There were other possibilities for action available to Chasid. Along with his work with teenage club groups, he might have organized parent committees to help with programs. After the parent committees were organized, a few subtle suggestions could have moved them to go to the director and offer their help with the total operation of the center. Having recruited the members for the committees, Chasid could have insured that some of the people would be interested in more than planning a summer picnic or a bus ride to the country.

It is, of course, possible that the director would stall and delay with the parent committees' request. But given the climate in the inner cities, and the fact that the CCC is a white-dominated organization, could there actually be a great deal of delay? One mention of going to the newspapers or picketing the central headquarters—"CCC discriminates against blacks and Puerto Ricans" —would probably bring immediate action. The director might also realize that in his struggle to maintain funds for the center, he would be in a much better position with a board of local people behind him than if he had to depend on the whims and vagaries of central staff.

This pressure strategy utilizes both the desire of CCC to maintain its prestige and status, and the desire of a division to insure its survival. At the same time, there are rewards to members of the division from the director on down: their jobs are more secure, their independence more viable. All of these levels of rewards and costs could have been activated by Chasid, a lower staff worker.

To get an agency to radically change its goals and programs is probably the most difficult task a line worker can undertake. The staff and the board are going to have to be won over. Perrow (1970, pp. 172–173) makes it abidingly clear what Chasid was up against with the administration and staff. "Goals become built into organizations, making change difficult . . . personnel who cannot adapt to the prevailing goals leave or find their advancement blocked; those who do adapt, recruit others of similar views . . . technical people are recruited for work on specific [programs], limiting the [agency's] ability to shift to other [activities] . . . in a sense, people do not resist change, but rather patterns of interaction, relationships, bargains, negotiations, mutual adjustments, and above all, forms of solutions or ways of handling problems resist change."

Likewise, at the board level, there is no good reason to assume that a board made up of poor people would be any more adaptable to program changes than a board made up of rich people. There are great differences amongst the people who live in slum areas. Surprisingly large numbers are middle-class oriented, if not actually middle-class in terms of education and income. There are those who are completely beaten down, hopeless, and there are those who simply need a chance. The program interests of all of these subgroups are by no means congruent.

In addition, poor people are just as prone to have a board dominated by one man, or a clique, to be subject to pet ideas, to be manipulated by a smart executive director, to be interested in maintaining status. The composition of the board, the expertise available to it, the time and commitment its members are willing to make, plus the attitude of the executive towards it, all affect its operation. It is conceivable, should Chasid have nurtured a board, that he could have been just as disappointed in them as he was in the new employment counselor.

Because they are more accessible, line workers generally attempt to involve staff in their ideas for change. Yet at some point boards will have to be considered since they have ultimate authority over agency policy. Subsequent chapters deal with the means of changing the procedures and composition of boards as well as with the means by which they can be made more accessible to staff and more responsive to community needs. These are difficult and complex tasks.

Discussion

History is influence. Every agency has a history of ways in which it has evaluated its success and run its programs. Each agency was started by particular people who wanted to achieve specific ends. If these people are still active, they may still have a great deal to say about what goes on in the agency.

To the extent possible, the worker should analyze the ways in which past experiences still affect agency practices. When, how, and why do changes take place? What was the most recent organizational change? Has the organization been operating in identical fashion for five or ten years? Some organizations change only when a new executive director comes. Others change like the seasons. Annual meeting reports, board meeting minutes, and older staff members can provide a great deal of such information.

Certain levels of agency hierarchies or departments are more dynamic than others. They have a history of grievances or shared commitments that can be activated for certain specific activities. Some departments even hate each other. Now assume that your agency must absorb a 15 percent budget cut. Which departments or staff would be cut or reduced? Had Chasid considered all of these questions, he might have approached CPU much more cautiously.

The first step in mapping a strategy of change is the anticipation of resistances. While resistances may have a variety of sources, they can be translated into a common denominator of rewards and costs. What costs are implied to individuals, departments and the organization as a whole? Will the potential rewards outweigh the costs?

While simple addition or subtraction of such complex factors is not possible, a listing of potential rewards and costs can be of considerable help in making judgments about the advisability of particular courses of action. As noted, Chasid's judgments were neither systematic nor well founded.

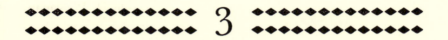

3

Changing Treatment Procedures

In developing schemes for change in treatment procedures workers soon learn that the mere assertion that a particular treatment "isn't working" seldom achieves much, even if there are certain facts to back up the assertion. The effectiveness of outcome statistics on bringing about changes in treatment patterns is dependent on the values and judgment of those who must make the change.

Is not recidivism a good index of the success of the criminal justice system? Not if you believe punishment is a deterrent to others who might be criminally inclined or if you believe the system should not be blamed for lack of jobs, public attitudes toward ex-prisoners, neighborhood environments, and the like. Yet if there is no agreed-upon standard of success, it is going to be difficult to enlist support for changes in treatment patterns. A common basis for discussion will not exist.

One reason why agencies seem to simultaneously pursue different standards of success is that they often exist with severe conflicts amongst their goals. A probation department must maintain custody of a parolee, insuring that he does not break the law. At the same time, the department must rehabilitate the parolee. If the public insists on extremely close surveillance and excessive restrictions on parolees, rehabilitative programs depending on the development of mutual trust may be subtly undermined as parole officers are forced to act more like policemen than social workers. The agency is, therefore, forced to balance itself carefully between custody and rehabilitation.

Probation department administrators feel that this balancing act is necessary to maintain the possibility of programs other than those of a custodial nature (Clark, 1961). Some parole officers, nevertheless, push their agencies toward the rehabilitation camp. In these efforts staff are often stymied because they lack a sense of timing as well as a sense of the difficulty of gaining agreement about what the agency can and should accomplish.

Scope of the Problem

Robert Beauchamps, a twenty-eight-year-old marine corps veteran, is employed in the downstate office of the Southern State Department of Probation. Beauchamps is tall and muscular and has a quiet, soft-spoken quality. Orphaned at fourteen, he spent several years in a public institution where he was influenced by a social worker named Williams. After his discharge from the Marine Corps, he entered the Tulane School of Social Work and received his M.S.W. in 1965.

The parole system in Beauchamps' state is quite complex. It is administered by a board of corrections. This board and the governor appoint the commissioner of corrections. It also appoints the parole boards for the adult and juvenile prisons. Real power over the prison system rests with the penal subcommittee at the state legislature. This subcommittee controls the money for the total operation of the system, and tends to cut what it considers to be the frills out of departmental budget requests. Although reform legislators have recently attempted to introduce rehabilitative programs into various aspects of the system, they are a distinct minority on the committee.

Beauchamps' office is relatively small; it includes a director, an assistant director, three supervisors, sixteen probation officers, and clerical staff. The juvenile parole division has increasingly hired M.S.W.s. The director of Beauchamps' office was an M.S.W., as were several of the supervisors. While only three of the parole officers had their M.S.W.s, others planned to go on to school. Cases are received either directly from the state reformatory (for sixteen- to twenty-one-year-old male offenders) or from the courts. First offenders are usually placed on probation. During his first two months on the job, Beauchamps was confused by the tremendous clash of attitudes and values about the appropriate treatment of parolees. Some workers believed that incarceration helped. Others pointed to the high rate of recidivism as proof that it did not.

Some parole officers wanted to establish a therapeutic relationship with the parolees. They sought ways to show their concern. Many workers tried to establish relationships, but felt that their power to send the parolee back to prison made such relationships suspect.

Some questioned whether a parolee/officer relationship was the central factor in rehabilitation. They suggested the use of ex-parolees, group counseling, or other alternatives to sending kids back to state institutions. Still others denied that the goal of helping parolees make an adequate adjustment in the community was realistic. They considered it criminal to encourage the parolees to adjust to the intolerable conditions in the neighborhoods in which they lived.

Older members of the department pointed out that no matter what was done, no matter what innovations had been introduced over the years, the recidivism rate varied little. Training schools get the children who have failed at all other institutions. Reform schools are in rural areas and do nothing to prepare the inmates for return to the large city. Finally, the budget determines the programs no matter what is best for the clients.

Beauchamps felt that his work was determined by a series of pressures. The caseload was too large. Therefore it had to be managed. Management was not easy because there actually were very few clear policies in the agency. For example, he could not get an adequate definition of a "parole violator." When he first

took the job, the state reformatories were full. It was quite clear
that there was a push on not to put parole violators back in jail. A
parole violation one month may not be considered a parole violation another month.

He also found that different parole officers treat violations in
different ways. Some look the other way when infractions are minor.
Other officers apply a basic rule, "If they act up, throw them in
the clink."

Beauchamps got little help from his supervisors. He quickly
discovered that they really did not want him to ask questions. They
saw themselves as protecting society rather than rehabilitating the
individual parolee. If both could be done, fine (Piven and Pappenfort, 1960).

Beauchamps wanted to establish relationships with the
parolees, but the large caseload prevented him from doing so.
Between getting basic information for the various reports they had
to fill out and the innumerable crises that occurred with each
client, parole officers had little time to plan a coherent program of
rehabilitation for any of the parolees. For example, workers were
always on call should a client find himself back in court. They
might have to spend a day waiting around for the case to be called.

The inability to control their own time lowered morale. It
made Beauchamps feel that he was not really controlling events;
rather, events were controlling him. The situation was summed up
by one of his colleagues, "No one ever says we appreciate your
efforts. Everyone is beaten down. We need some kind of feedback.
You don't get it from the kids, and if you do, you are never sure
you really helped. It might have been someone or something else."

Without some standard of success for the department, confusion and frustration would inevitably continue. There was no way
of telling who or what was right or wrong. This confusion has un-
fortunate consequences for parole officer performance. The line
workers are cheated out of a feeling of success. Instead, they adapt
to failure.

Resistance to Change

The director of the regional office, Simpson, had worked
in the probation department for twenty years. Six years ago he had

been sent to a school of social work. Simpson was a bright man. He was aware of the many problems in the department, but he knew the difficulties the central office was having with the legislature. He was also aware of the limitations of many of the supervisors and staff members.

Simpson's main problem, which he could not discuss with the staff, was his own immediate supervisor, a man who refused to take any responsibility. Because Simpson had to assume a great deal of his supervisor's authority, he could be vulnerable in a shake-up.

Many executive directors like Simpson maintain an open door policy. Lower level staff may come and speak to the director any time they feel that it is appropriate. There are problems with this policy, however. It alters the lines of communication in the agency. It alerts supervisory staff that something is wrong and can give them a sense of insecurity. The director must consider the ramifications of his actions on the total staff. If he were to change the entire agency following one person's complaint, then that one person becomes quite powerful.

Beauchamps complained that he did not have time to see his clients, that he was not developing his professional skills, and that the agency was removed from the communities where the parolees lived. After only three months, Beauchamps was telling a man who had spent twenty years in the department what was wrong. Just that morning Simpson had stuck his neck out by refusing to sign a return to custody order from a particularly punitive parole officer.

Simpson thought that Beauchamps was sincere, yet young and immature. Even though he wanted a staff that was concerned and willing to protest, he decided to give Beauchamps a bureaucratic lesson. He did so not out of malice, but because he felt that Beauchamps had a rather abstract view of what the job was. While he had very human feelings for the clients, Beauchamps displayed no such feelings for his co-workers, the administration, or the public in general.

Simpson asked Beauchamps how many of his cases he had seen more than once a week. Beauchamps was startled: "How could I possibly have time to see them more than once a week?" Simpson responded that when he had been a parole officer, he had often worked nights along with his fellow officers. This, of course, was true. He did not mention that then the office had only four men and that there was a fantastic sense of camaraderie because they had been building something new and important.

When Beauchamps mentioned the paper work, Simpson asked if he had attempted to figure out ways to make it less onerous. Beauchamps felt that this was not possible. Simpson did not think it was that bad. Simpson suggested that Beauchamps come back and see him in a month or so, for another discussion. The interview was over, and Beauchamps left feeling that he had been talking to a blank wall.

Beauchamps described his conversation with Simpson to friends in the office. In the grumbling that followed, someone suggested doing a questionnaire among themselves. One worker with some knowledge of research methods wrote up a questionnaire, and twelve of the fifteen parole officers filled it out. The questions did not pertain to individuals, but to the work and procedures of the total department. No names were taken. Beauchamps' friend then tabulated all of the responses and wrote a summary of the report. Next, they set up an audience with Simpson, suggesting that a staff meeting be held for the entire office to discuss the results of the questionnaire.

Neither were prepared for the hostility of Simpson. He asked them what their research competence was and suggested that the questions were biased. Then he asked why this had not been cleared with their supervisors first. While he agreed to call a staff meeting, he did not want the research questionnaire results distributed until the research director from the state office commented on the procedures and bias of the questions.

The meeting with Simpson occurred on June 1. When the new budget came down on July 1, the number of open slots for parole officer II had been reduced. Beauchamps' friend had only a provisional appointment as a parole officer II, so he was demoted back to beginning parole officer.

Some of the workers blamed the system. "The system is paranoid. They believe that the problems did not exist prior to the study. The study made the problems." Of course, Simpson knew all about the problems. He was concerned that this written statement in the form of a research study could get into the wrong hands if it were circulated. There were people in the department anxious to use any bit of information to promote their own ends by leaking it to the legislature, anxious to frustrate attempts to introduce more rehabilitation and less control into the program.

A Do-Good Organizational Secret: What seems good for the clients is not necessarily good for the agency.

After the demotion of Beauchamps' friend, the younger parole officers felt that they had to force the administration to take the actions necessary to improve the office. The staff meeting held on September 20 was tumultuous. Simpson brought an assistant director for program planning from the central office. Workers complained that they were treated like dirt. "There is not even the courtesy of an acknowledgment of our suggestions." The administration waved the ghost of the budget, placing the blame on the legislature which simply does not understand us. One of the older workers admitted that "Perhaps we scapegoat the administration because we are frustrated by lack of success with the clients."

Finally, Simpson agreed to an all-day workshop to develop specific recommendations for dealing with the problems. There was also an immediate need for a clearly written manual of procedures. A steering committee was appointed including both workers and administrators to plan for the workshop and develop the policy manual. The chairman of the steering committee was a young parole officer. Therefore, it seemed as if a significant step had been made in sharing control in the agency.

The all-day workshop was held on November 20 at a local conference center. There were four workgroups. Each met for three hours and was followed by a plenary session. An implementing committee was set up after the meeting to work on several of the specific suggestions. The chairman of the steering committee and Simpson became the cochairmen of the implementing committee. It became clear at the workshop that there was a difference in perspective among the staff concerning the definition of the worker's role as a helper, the definition of effective service, and the nature of the parolee's participation in the workings of the agency. Beauchamps and his friends felt that the implementing committee could work around these problems in setting priorities.

Somehow, whenever Beauchamps and his friends discuss

the events that transpired after November 20, there is always a hazy feeling about just what occurred. One thing is definite. November 20 is referred to by all as the "one-day high." Some say that the administration co-opted the implementing committee, perverting its policy-setting purpose through overattention to detail. Others say that the real problem occurred when the activist cochairman left the agency for a higher paying job. In any case, because there was a committee, working people lost interest. There was nothing for them to do during the long periods of committee deliberation.

Beauchamps felt that he could not call the committee to account. When he complained about specifics, other staff would tell him that he did not know all the facts. He concluded that the ramifications of conflict—including reprisals—are too great to easily sustain an insurgent movement based on the power of line staff.

Simpson was fond of saying that an agency is no democracy. Beauchamps and his friends felt that a good administration involves the staff in making decisions because the staff has a great deal of information and knowledge. Yet, they seemed unwilling to admit that there was a need for accountability in the agency. Simpson, for his part, underestimated the staff's desire to participate (Wilcox, 1969).

Beauchamps and his friends were a little weak on English history. The Magna Carta was not a victory for democracy, it was a victory for the barons. Ultimately, democracy benefited. If wicked King John is to be tamed, he will not be tamed by an unorganized group of workers whose interests are often in conflict. He will probably be tamed by the supervisors on whom he must depend. In addition, these supervisors have ways of confounding the workers— promotions, transfers, evaluations, reference letters, choice assignments, and a variety of indulgences.

Could the barons have been organized in Beauchamps' office? It seems highly unlikely. Had they all been professionals with M.S.W.s, they might have had a shared value system which could have served as a counterweight to excessive identification with the bureaucratic needs of the department. But even then it is not always possible because of individual personalities and desires. In all likelihood the one-day high for the workers was a one-day low for the supervisors. Beauchamps and his friends had missed the emotional element of work. The supervisors had worked their way up to their positions, and they did not want workers telling them what to do.

Strategy

The state legislature had a great impact on the operation of the Department of Probation. This impact was centered in the legislative subcommittee on prisons and parole. One of the members of the subcommittee was a liberal legislator from the area. Surprisingly, almost no line workers and few directors of regional offices knew all the members of this subcommittee. While some states prohibit public employees from engaging in certain types of political activity, these rules and regulations are generally ambiguous and not enforced. Because state legislators seldom have a great deal of money to run their campaigns, they depend on volunteers. Beauchamps volunteered to help the liberal state legislator get reelected.

Such a personal contact can be both valuable and dangerous. Obviously, ideas and information can be communicated directly to the legislator. However, once it is known in the agency that such a personal contact exists, there is a tendency for administration to tread warily. A sophisticated administration can keep information from the worker and in so doing insulate itself. Nevertheless, this lever should certainly be within the line worker's arsenal.

A Do-Good Organizational Secret: When conflicts exist between organizational mission and organizational maintenance, most agencies will compromise their mission.

Beauchamps reasoned that agency administrators will risk legislative censure over innovative rehabilitative programs only with considerable public support for the programs. A climate of concern for parolees has to be created. Political office holders can provide a forum for the creation of such concerns.

Constant battling with the legislature over the budget and frustration at the lack of success in reaching professed goals built a great deal of defensiveness into the agency. After a year on the job, Beauchamps realized that his whole approach to change in this agency might have been wrong. The more he attacked the resistances head on, the more the resistances hardened. He was amazed at how obvious this was. He would never attack a parolee's resistances head on.

Beauchamps came to see that there was a certain authority granted to competence. If you can really do your job, other people respect you and give you quite a bit of leeway. Beauchamps decided that he could use this leeway to encourage and assist others, not so much to help others, but to assure them that his hard work was not for personal gain. This informal power could then be used to build trust which would help overcome some resistances to change. He had by this time decided that Simpson was indeed a very capable man and a potential ally. Not every regional office, of course, is so blessed.

Beauchamps also realized that he had one other plus. The regional office was comparatively small; there were only twenty-five people in the entire office. Everyone was known by his first name. There was good potential for getting a great deal of the work done in an informal manner rather than through bureaucratic policies and procedures (Blau, 1955).

Friday afternoons were slow times in the agency. Workers often used the time to gripe. On one Friday afternoon, a secretary had a birthday and the other girls brought a cake into the office. This gave Beauchamps an idea. The next Friday afternoon Beauchamps brought a cake. He and five or six of the workers sat in the conference room and talked about one of Beauchamps' parolees who was clearly headed back to prison. Gradually over the months, the number of workers attending increased. Then some of the clerical staff joined the group. Surprisingly, they had a lot to say about some of the cases. Simpson began dropping in, and after about six months the conferences became an established ritual in the office. Informal peer supervision had transpired without any administrative edict or discussion. Shared responsibility was being created.

Discussion

Beauchamps' ultimate goal was to get the office to informally think about the results of its work. He hoped that at some point the

Friday afternoon meetings would turn to talk about what actually happens to all the clients. Ultimately such discussions might lead to experimentation with new procedures. Certainly the research questionnaire, the all-day staff meeting, and the confrontations had been poorly timed. Their effectiveness rested on trust which had not been developed. Therefore they failed.

Any change in a social agency will involve a certain amount of risk to status, job security, friendships, and chances of promotion. Also, it is not always clear that the proposed change will result in the promised reward. Something above and beyond logical argument is required. Trust in the proponent of change can often make risk-taking possible. Yet, the situation in many agencies makes it impossible to develop trust.

Beauchamps' situation was more promising. He hoped to develop a feedback system of information that would alert his office to potential changes and alterations in procedures. Lack of such a system compounded chaos: suspicion among levels of staff, animosity with the legislature, no sense of the worthwhileness of the job, fear of public accountability, and ritualistic procedures.

This chaos developed over time through the interplay of a complicated set of factors: desire to get increased funds, unsubstantiated beliefs in the usefulness of particular ways of helping people, vested interests in job security, the public's desire to feel something is being done, too much work for too few staff, the strains between various goals, and the problems of defining indices of success.

Why was chaos allowed to develop in the department? Who could have stopped it? The administrators faced a hostile legislative committee. Even if they had ideas based on the facts, experience showed they could not get the legislature to vote more money, or other parts of the system, such as the prisons, to change their procedures. The legislative committee had no independent way of assessing the work of the department and felt they were dealing with budget padders similar to those in any other department. With such a situation, over a period of time survival becomes the agency's creed.

There is, unfortunately, no basis to assume that merely gathering facts will have much effect. The significant question is who gathers the facts, and what they do with them. Line staff must be concerned not only with what the administration knows, but also with what a board knows.

Beauchamps and his friends attempted to get the facts, but the agency could not really utilize them. Their timing was off.

Facts can only be a source of influence when boards are so structured as to seriously carry out their accountability functions. Boards of directors of private agencies are empowered to set agency policy. Few public agencies have boards with such powers, however. One board of corrections for a whole state can hardly oversee a whole prison and parole system.

In public agencies, boards must have broad representation if they are to be effective: representatives of different political parties, the media, religious and professional groups, as well as the recipients of the service. The truth is more likely to come out when such diverse interests are brought into play.

While facts can be a catalyst for change, the indices of success which an agency utilizes affect its evaluation of these facts. Beauchamps initially missed this point. He assumed certain standards which were not fully operative. The recidivism rate was not really the basis upon which it judged its effectiveness.

Read an annual report. Some agencies stress their professionalism: consultants, new projects, training apparatus, and speeches delivered. Others stress program efforts: so many clients served, so much money distributed. Some talk a great deal about program efficiency: "We are now serving two hundred more clients at half the cost." A few talk about results: "The rate of recidivism among our clients is 35 percent."

Agencies usually have informal standards of success. To discover these standards, ascertain why people were fired or where the administration puts pressure on staff. Once discovered, these informal standards must be called into question if they blunt serious consideration of agency effectiveness. (See *Chapter 7* for a technical discussion of agency effectiveness.) This is what Beauchamps began to do at the Friday afternoon Koffee Klatches.

Beauchamps was wise to attempt to influence the department from without as well as from within. There are many groups outside the agency who are concerned about agency standards.

However, other agencies, client groups, public interest groups of a political or social nature, and funding sources can also cause problems. Many such groups are only too willing to use information provided by staff for their own purposes. Simpson was rightly concerned about Beauchamps' research. Not everyone is dedicated to truth. Birth control is a genocide plot, mental health is a communist conspiracy, counseling diverts people from political activism. A good deal of agency insistence on going through channels is to protect itself against such eventualities.

While Beauchamps and his friends too quickly decided not to go through channels and to stick their necks out, experience indicates that in many situations, someone has to stick his neck out if any change is to occur. "Legitimation for these efforts is derived from the practitioner's ethical obligation to place professional values above organizational allegiance" (Patti and Resnick, 1972, p. 48). If adopted at the extreme, this point of view would give license to any worker to do anything he considered in the client's best interest. Yet it is not all so clear what the client's best interest is. In addition, what one may do in the interest of one set of clients may be inimical to the interests of another set of clients.

Yet following channels can be a magnificent defense for the status quo. For balance, there must be risk for avoiding channels. The consequences which comprise the risk make it less likely that only one set of interests and concerns will be taken into account by organizational actors. They also make it more likely that the rash, the immature, the power hungry, and the self-serving can be contained. These people will clothe their personal concerns in moral arguments about client's needs.

When sticking one's neck out, the turtle rather than Marie Antoinette is the appropriate model. Timing is crucial. Had there been public concern and support for innovation by local politicians and citizens, Beauchamps' friend probably would not have been demoted.

Some staff are better situated for risk-taking than others. Past services to the organization, professional reputation, and personal contacts make them less vulnerable. They are also likely to be more effective in making the administration listen to what they are saying.

Sometimes going through channels can be a way of stepping over them. Periodically when their grievances mount, policemen have been known to meticulously enforce every law on the books. The ensuing outcry often gets them what they want. Following sensitive procedures ritualistically can achieve the same results in social agencies. Yet, staff should anticipate administrative anger which usually devolves into an attempt to get the ringleaders.

There are, of course, some battles which must be fought even though one expects to lose. The history of most significant changes is the history of initial defeats. How to leave one's job and have an organizational impact is an important consideration (Nader, Petkas, and Blackwell, 1972).

4

Dealing with Incompetent Supervisors

A common diagnosis of agency ills is incompetence. Some people cannot perform their jobs. Yet, replacement will not necessarily change anything. The new person may be as bad or worse than the former, the structure and procedures of the agency may be more the cause of problems than the incompetence of individuals, or the goals of the organization may be so incompatible that no one can really function effectively.

Despite these factors, the diagnosis is often accurate. Incompetence can be a major bottleneck in any organization. The problem for line staff is how to get rid of that bottleneck. Indeed, staff often spend a great deal of time discussing and planning what should be done. It is especially frustrating that their first hand information and knowledge about the nature of the incompetency cannot be effectively used to get the incompetent individual replaced.

There are quite a few reasons for this. One relates to the unique relationships, especially in casework supervision. Casework supervisors are responsible for helping caseworkers improve their skills and for evaluating and administratively helping them do the job. While these supervising functions are common to other professions, there is a difference. Casework supervisors focus their attention on workers' awareness and understanding of their own motivations and feelings, as these can affect the workers' ability to be of help to troubled clients.

Yet, because the supervisor decides whether the worker gets a positive evaluation, the worker is not likely to admit his innermost feelings and difficulties with the job to the supervisor (Scherz, 1958). And, if he does, it is easy to evaluate any complaints as symptoms of psychological problems. Yet one can have personality difficulties and still assess an organization accurately.

The strains in the supervisor's role belie any simple solution. Unfortunately, the problems are compounded in social agencies by lack of supervisor training. Line workers who have performed well are simply promoted to the position of supervisor after a period of years. Often this works well. However, a talented caseworker does not necessarily make a talented supervisor.

Lower level staff most acutely feel their lack of influence in agencies when their supervisors are less than competent. Maria Hanrahan quickly found this out when she took a position as a family counselor in the Brookville regional office of Christian Charities.

Scope of the Problem

Christian Charities offers a wide range of services including family counseling, homemaker services, a sheltered workshop, day and overnight camping, a variety of recreational programs, plus health care in a multimillion dollar complex of hospitals. Each year, public fund-raising campaigns are held. Technically, the director of the charitable endeavors is the head of the church. There is no actual board of directors, although there is an advisory board for fund-raising. Policy-making is in the hands of an army of controllers, staff planners, consultants, and directors and associate directors for the various divisions all housed at the Charities' central office.

The Brookville office is fairly similar to the other offices, even though it is the largest. It includes a director, an assistant director, two supervisors, ten case workers (most of whom have M.S.W.s), four homemakers, and a public health nurse. Maria Hanrahan was one of the case workers.

The director and the assistant director are ordained clergymen and professionally trained social workers. Most of the administrative hierarchy in family services of Christian Charities, like the director and assistant director in the Brookville office, have their M.S.W.s. Yet, the style of administration mirrors that of the church, hierarchically oriented with clear lines of authority and a distinct tradition of accepting orders given by a superior. Even more so than the Cooperative Community Centers, the hierarchy of CC expect to spend their lives in the organization. This tends to buttress the acceptance of authority.

Reverence for authority is especially pronounced in Brookville. The attitude of the director—"do it because I say you should do it"—overshadows the staff meetings completely. Changes seem to come from on-high rather than from staff discussion.

Procedures are similar to those of any family agency in the country. An intake section interviews clients and presents the cases for disposition at a case conference run by the assistant director. Members of the staff have an opportunity to comment at the conference. Both parents, only the children, or the whole family may be seen for weekly interviews. There is no one prescribed treatment formulation, although most of the caseworkers are trained in ego psychology. The goals of the agency are quite broad. It focuses on family stability, and anything which would promote this end is considered appropriate.

The agency has been housed in the same building for forty-five years. It seems generally oblivious to the changes which have occurred in Brookville during this time. Its services have remained the same while the ethnic composition of the borough has shifted largely to Puerto Rican and Black.

During high school, Maria Hanrahan had considered entering a religious order but decided against it. She spent a few years as a secretary, then began going to college at night. After graduating from college at twenty-seven, Maria taught school for several years. She was an exceptional teacher, especially with children whom other teachers had stamped as incorrigible. Students were often transferred to Maria's class. Her work with the guidance counselors in the school brought her into contact with social workers who encouraged her to get her master's degree.

The job as family counselor was Maria's first upon graduation. She was shocked at the comparatively low level of practice at the agency. Some workers' case presentations seemed to be at the beginning graduate student level. Her supervisor, Ms. Bowden, gave most of her attention to statistical counts—the number of interviews held per week and the number of collateral calls made. After three months, Maria had learned nothing at all about treatment in the weekly conferences.

Ms. Bowden was not anxious to make innovations. Maria suggested that an experiment be attempted with group therapy for parents of children with similar behavior problems. Ms. Bowden first ignored the request, then agreed to talk it over with the assistant director. When pressed, Ms. Bowden explained that the assistant director did not think that it was feasible at this time. Maria was sure that it had never been adequately discussed with the assistant director, but she could not challenge Ms. Bowden's statement.

Resistance to Change

Over the months, Maria made several friends in the agency. They had had similar experiences with Ms. Bowden and explained their techniques of dealing with her.

Playing the game involves giving lip service to whatever the supervisor wants, but actually doing what you want on your own. "She talked a lot about herself. I had to go along and listen if I wanted to get a good evaluation. I did not have time to waste on this. If I tried to focus the conference, it was often interpreted as hostility." Playing the game enables the worker to do what he thinks best, but does not solve his problem of getting the kind of supervision that will help him improve his capacity as a worker.

One tactic for dealing with incompetency is direct confrontation. The worker carefully documents cases of poor practice on the part of the supervisor. Sometimes several workers do this together. At times, the dossier is presented to the assistant director or the executive director of the agency; at other times the supervisor is confronted directly. Seldom does confrontation work in the manner in which it is hoped. Sometimes workers are accused of having authority problems; other times they are accused of unprofessional activity for being overzealous in compiling a dossier.

Two years ago, a worker overheard Ms. Bowden discussing her with a client. As the walls are paper thin between offices, she could not help but hear. Ms. Bowden mentioned to the client that this particular worker was overinvolved with her cases. The worker, incensed, involved two other workers. Together they went to the executive director. Three days later, they were all fired for unprofessional behavior. Communication between worker and client is sacrosanct. Of course, Ms. Bowden said they had misinterpreted the conversation.

Administration almost always backs up supervisors in a confrontation with a worker. Not to do so often means that the supervisor must be fired. If the worker can have the supervisor overruled, the authority of that supervisor is undermined and his effectiveness may be diminished. It is much easier to replace a worker than a supervisor.

Some workers learn to be devious. After giving lip service to a supervisor and building up a reputation for competence, they begin to maneuver for a transfer to another supervisor. This is seldom done on the basis of dissatisfaction with the supervisor. To do so makes the granting of the transfer subject to an agreement that the supervisor is bad. A pretext is used. "Supervisor Y is experimenting with behavior therapies. I have worked hard and I want to increase my knowledge. I deserve to be given that transfer and the opportunity."

The transfer often requires a period of negotiation. The

worker intimates that perhaps he should look for another job. The agency makes a variety of objections. It is finally agreed that for a period of time, worker X will be transferred to supervisor Y. In most cases, this transfer is quite permanent. The technique works for worker X, but does very little for the other workers in the unit. Everyone cannot transfer.

There is currently much interest in peer supervision in family agencies. Instead of a weekly conference with the supervisor, there is a weekly conference of all the workers. Cases are presented, options of treatment are discussed, and errors are pointed out. This technique is a good means of working around a poor supervisor. Peer supervision requires a motivated and knowledgeable staff and, more importantly, a supervisor who is willing to give up a good deal of control. Nevertheless, some workers need individual supervision (Wax, 1959).

Strategy

Maria's greatest asset was her ability to develop a clear picture of the capabilities and limitations of her co-workers. Several of these workers needed close supervision. Yet, some of them were the most vehement critics of the supervisor. Two actually left shortly after Maria came to the agency. One explained that whenever she went for a job interview, she simply said that she was leaving because she had a personality conflict with the supervisor. It was obvious to Maria that such a description covered up more than it revealed. The problem would require a better definition, one that could lead to some resolution.

A supervisor, just as any other worker, must justify his existence in the agency; he must show others just what it is that he does and why it is important. For Ms. Bowden, this meant keeping her unit running smoothly. To do this she felt she had to know every detail of each worker's activities.

It can also be expected that a supervisor will so define his job so that he spends the vast majority of his time doing those aspects of the job that he can do well, and underplaying those aspects in which he is less able and less secure. Ms. Bowden derived a great deal of satisfaction from compiling reports, keeping statistics, and maintaining relations with other social agencies. She definitely was not the type of supervisor who could derive satisfaction from helping others develop and grow. She was quite incapable of creating this type of atmosphere.

Ms. Bowden wanted to become an assistant director and eventually a director of a family agency. She felt that she had to please the administration of the Brookville center. In her appraisal, the staff were the natives and the administration did not want the natives to be restless.

The workers complained, "She won't go to bat for us." Whether it was a personal problem or an idea for a new program or a procedure, the staff felt that Ms. Bowden would never advocate for them with the administration. She did not seem able to back them up. This was most infuriating, as it gave the staff a sense of impotence and helplessness.

There are specific emotional pressures on supervisors which become quite apparent on the job. Some case workers take a job as a supervisor simply because it pays more money and offers higher status. They are completely floored by the necessity to exercise authority, are uncomfortable about saying no, and cannot bring themselves to fire even the most incompetent of workers. On the other hand, there are those, such as Ms. Bowden, who are always checking up lest their authority be in some mysterious way weakened.

Some supervisors want everyone to love them. Their decisions seem arbitrary because they are really based on feelings of love and rejection, rather than on the merits of the case. Such supervisors often want their immediate superiors to love them. This is a dangerous and sad affair. The staff are the unwanted children.

Discomfort with hostility is a disabling weakness for a supervisor. A boss will get a lot of heat whether in a social agency or in a sanitation department. When a supervisor cannot handle hostility, every question is interpreted potentially as a hostile act. Woe to the worker who does not realize this (Berliner, 1971).

Perhaps the most common problem of supervisors is the inability to let go, the problem of control. Ms. Bowden interfered in every case. Workers began to wonder whether it was really her case or theirs. Of course, not all supervisors have to control all the time, just as they do not always want love. A good clue to what a supervisor will attempt to control is what a supervisor must do to get a promotion.

If she wanted to stay with the agency, Maria had four options. She could do nothing, she could work around Ms. Bowden, she could attempt to have her fired, or she could help her do her job. Doing nothing was simply not acceptable. Working around Ms. Bowden seemed a last resort. Maria was concerned about the effectiveness of the agency and rightly saw that this solution could help her personally, but would do very little for the problem of inadequate direction in the agency.

Getting Ms. Bowden fired seemed difficult; the administration liked the way she ran the unit. Maria was also aware that administrators protect each other in relations with the staff, even though privately they may have great misgivings about one another.

How does administration know whether a supervisor is doing a good or bad job? There are obvious problems in the staff simply telling the administration, from being suspected of wanting the supervisor's job, to having authority problems, to risking being fired. If the assistant director does not attend case conferences, how will he ever know that the level of practice is poor? How will he ever get the idea that Ms. Bowden is an incompetent teacher? Opening up sources of data to the administration is vital so that they can form their own judgment without the staff's prompting.

In dealing with an incompetent supervisor, one must know what supervisors can be fired for. In some agencies they cannot be fired; all they have to do is be there from nine to five. At times, workers assist supervisors in covering up inadequacies simply because they have things to cover up as well. A critical incident can supply an opportunity to uncover reality for the administration. Of course, what is a critical incident to the staff may not be so critical to the administration.

There is nothing unethical about this line of action. Entrapment is not being suggested. Rather, if certain events occur, their potential ramifications must be brought to the attention of the administration. Administrators must be able to justify firing. Once access to information about a supervisor has been opened up for the administration, then documentation and confrontation by the staff can have much more effect. Firing is a serious administrative step. Staff can succeed in getting administration to evaluate this possibility by engaging in a process of increasing pressure. First, open up direct access to information for administration. Second, submit reports and documentation from staff.

Administrators are always much more impressed by reports from staff who have a reputation for competence. Often when they leave the agency, such staff can request a conference with top administrative staff and specify the nature of a specific individual's incompetence. Some staff have to be encouraged to do this. The cumulative effect of a variety of such reports can be important. Yet more pressure may be needed.

Opening up contacts with outside concerned groups can provide pressure. Maria discovered that the local parish priests were upset with the imperious way Ms. Bowden handled requests for services for their parishoners. Some of the priests did not agree with the type of service the agency was offering. A simple suggestion from Maria could have galvanized the discontent into group action at the board level.

Additional pressure can then be applied by such a group contacting state and national standard-setting bodies, such as an association of family agencies. While credentialling groups seldom concern themselves with the competence of individuals and are not particularly effective in enforcing standards, they do have a nuisance value in an escalating process of bringing pressure to bear. Others can initiate such contacts more easily than staff, who would be accused of not going through channels. Administration may be looking for an out and should not be given one by staff.

Administrations may be aware of a problem, but will do nothing about it. If such is the case, then the question is why the administration will do nothing. The answer will tell what, if anything, can be done. For example, many incompetent high level people are not fired because they have good relationships with funding sources. Executives are loathe to upset these relationships. Staff had best be aware of such situations.

Maria decided that she should not try to have Ms. Bowden fired. Given the administration of the agency, replacement might not be any better and could be worse. It also seemed debatable whether the problem was really Ms. Bowden or the total operation of the agency. Perhaps in the long run Ms. Bowden would have to go; yet, a more appropriate place to start was the balance of power between the workers and the supervisor.

Maria decided to pressure Ms. Bowden and the administration to do their jobs. The balance of power between the workers and the supervisor needed correcting. Supervisors have a variety of powerful tools with which to control workers. These tools include promotions, salary increases, and indulgences. Indulgences, created by relaxing certain rules, are the most subtle and effective. Relaxing the rules about coming in by nine, finishing one's dictation before going away on vacation, vacation time, caseload, and night work can create obligations which make it difficult to unite the staff against the supervisor (Gouldner, 1954, pp. 157–180).

Some supervisors engage in ammunition-gathering. Anything a worker does out of the ordinary is a problem. If a worker spends ten minutes more with a client, it is noted. If he comes in late, it is noted. Inferences are made about his interaction with other staff members. Casual comments over lunch are questioned. This ammunition is used at the worker's evaluation conference. One of Maria's co-workers was presented with such a dossier at her yearly evaluation. She was outraged, but realized that a show of anger would also be used against her. Ms. Bowden asked her why she was not upset. The worker coldly responded, "If I got angry, you'd say I was out of control."

Although it is not always possible or feasible to have a worker fired, it is often possible to transfer him to an undesirable place. Because of shifts in population, an additional worker is needed in Siberia, and it just happens that the supervisor has a worker available.

Discussion

The ultimate goal in redressing the balance of power is to create a system of supervision and evaluation from the bottom up as well as from the top down. Such a change is not easily instituted. Of course, there now are precedents for it in the universities with students evaluating faculty.

Most workers are not willing to criticize their supervisors for fear of reprisal. Therefore, the manner of the evaluation is important. Questioning the content and skill desired of supervision would be better than asking how good or bad Ms. Bowden is as a supervisor.

In large agencies, supervisors often protect each other. Therefore, information obtained from workers might not be utilized any more than the information traditionally discussed at staff evaluations. A board that actually holds the agency accountable is necessary. If an agency does not achieve its goals, information about internal functioning becomes quite relevant. The director has to seriously consider his staff problems because he could be fired. Supervisors like Ms. Bowden are then more likely to be called to task.

A Do-Good Organizational Secret: Agencies avoid consideration of their efficiency and effectiveness by focusing on the efficiency and effectiveness of their employees.

When there is accountability for results achieved, the irrationality of evaluating workers and agency at different times becomes apparent. In most agencies, workers receive yearly evaluations on the anniversary of their hiring date. This procedure has major limitations.

Separate evaluation results in an overemphasis on the worker's skills and an underemphasis on the part that agency structure and procedure play in his work. The agency may need to change its structure rather than increase supervision and staff training. This could be missed if the agency is not looking at itself at the same time it is looking at its workers.

The environment in which the agency operates—physical, social, financial—affects the worker's efforts. To tell the worker to refine his skills or work harder in order to be successful is to ignore the impact of environment. The caseload or lack of cooperation from other agencies, not diagnostic or therapeutic skills, may be at fault.

Evaluating individuals at different times during the year solely in terms of their individual therapeutic skills makes it less likely that the agency will have to react as a system to the results of the evaluations. The problems of each worker can be viewed idiosyncratically. The agency thus exhibits the classic client defense,

separation of one aspect of life from another. Evaluating workers'
ability to carry out therapeutic processes is worthless if the processes
are defective.

One final point about supervisors deserves mention. An incompetent supervisor can be a terrible stumbling block to securing a
promotion. Because an agency sees through its hierarchical structure, a line worker whose supervisor keeps him in the shadows must
devise alternative ways to be seen. Getting on interdepartmental
committees, writing articles, and becoming active in the local
chapter of NASW are all ways of increasing visibility. The worker
must be seen and known by the supervisor's supervisors. Agency
program planning and evaluation committees are excellent structures for achieving this end. If one is really determined, involvement
in fund-raising and agency public relations activities are even
better. Once the supervisors have seen you, they will find it harder
to deny you what you have earned.

In a more defensive tactic, the worker turns the focus of the
initial interview to supervision. He obtains in writing the goals of
supervision and the indices by which these goals will be judged.
This prevents supervisors from introducing items for evaluation
which have not been previously discussed.

Through consultation with experienced workers, agencies
should establish the areas of skill needing improvement and the
basis upon which to judge improvement—recordings, observations,
client queries, and the like. The worker should choose how to get
help, whether through conferences with the supervisor, through
taking courses, through peer supervision, or through consultation.
Letting the worker decide reduces the dependency feelings which
develop through forced supervision.

A degree of arbitrariness will always exist unless an agency
has some method of appraising success with clients. Without agency
standards of success and an evaluation of the worker's record,
workers and supervisors are dependent on secondary data. Case
presentation becomes more important than the people treated. The
way one writes or speaks about a case becomes more important than
the results achieved.

The key to increasing the influence of lower level staff vis-a-
vis their superiors lies in a board that can hold the agency account-

able. Where there is real accountability, the ideas and experience of all levels of staff become valuable, and the incompetence of individuals becomes a matter of serious concern.

If a board discovers that 80 percent of the agency's clients feel they have not been helped by the agency, then incompetent supervisors have something to worry about.

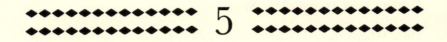

5

Making Boards Responsive

Besides providing information about the role boards of directors can play in bringing about change, this chapter has one other intent. It illustrates a number of traps that can ensnare workers in their efforts to make large agency systems work more effectively. The effort to gain acceptance of an innovation often leaves workers exhausted and unprepared for the problems of its implementation. Innovations if viewed as panaceas can result in situations no better, and often worse, than what existed prior to their implementation. The ability to modify plans on the basis of experience is crucial.

Social workers frequently complain that the *system* does not work. Such complaints cover the gamut from confused procedures to conflicting goals to departmental infighting, and are frequently heard in schools and hospitals where social workers offer supportive service to the institution. Because supportive staff suffer most from confusion in such systems and have the least influence to change them, they frequently agitate for change.

Scope of the Problem

In the 1960s, decentralization and local control of schools was widely espoused by social workers as a cure for system malaise. Barbara Hunter, a parent experienced with local school boards, was one of the few school social workers who urged caution with this approach. Nevertheless, she was not one to acquiesce to the status quo.

In 1960, Barbara was hired as a social worker for a large suburban school district. Her job and that of the other school social workers was to diagnose and treat children with behavior and learning problems. Barbara's first battle with the central administration of the Bureau of Child Guidance of the Board of Education occurred in September 1961.

During that year, the BCG switched from a policy of assigning staff only to schools needing special services to a policy of coverage for all schools in the system. This change in policy occurred without any change in the number of school social workers. The resulting pressure forced Barbara to ignore treatment and concentrate on diagnosis and referral.

The Bureau of Child Guidance operates out of the central Board of Education office. The chief of BCG reports directly to an assistant superintendent in charge of student services. BCG is one of many specialized departments under the operation of the Board of Education.

Funds for BCG come directly from the school budget. There is intense competition with other departments, such as health education and recreation, for allocations. The last major expansion in BCG occurred in the late 1950s in response to the multiproblem families concept. There has been almost no expansion since.

Each region of this school system is headed by a deputy superintendent and contains ten to fifteen elementary and high schools. BCG organized itself in exactly the same manner, but without maintaining regional offices. Supervision for each region is handled by supervisors housed at the central board offices. Barbara was one of five school social workers assigned to Region 4, the largest region.

Following the shiftover to total coverage of all schools, Barbara became virtually a free agent. Three of the principals in whose schools she worked had only the vaguest idea of what she was supposed to do. The central BCG office did not attempt to set priorities because there were so many children with problems. Thus, Barbara could do pretty much what she wanted. In fact, no one would know if she did nothing at all.

By instituting the new coverage policy, BCG had, in fact, lost control of the workers. One of Barbara's colleagues kept a very small caseload of ten to fifteen children to whom he gave intensive in-depth psychotherapy. He also made referrals to outside agencies. Other social workers gave no treatment at all and merely did diagnostic workups and referrals. And others organized groups of guidance teachers and trained them to do diagnosis and elementary types of counseling.

BCG lost control of its workers because each school in the school system is primarily a fief of its principal. Most principals operate as if they are kings. Their word is law. Leadership of BCG simply was not strong enough or interested enough to exert pressure on individual principals. Since its inception in the early 1950s, BCG has seen itself as an easily severed appendage. Thus, the social workers felt they had no way of affecting the school system.

When things go wrong, some are easily blamed. When children misbehave or do not learn, the school must account for it. Teachers blame the parents or the community, social workers blame the teachers, the principal blames the central administration and its policies, and the parents blame the system.

Many social workers criticize teachers for not understanding children, lacking sensitivity, or just being hostile. However, Barbara had a profound respect for the efforts of teachers. She had children of her own and felt that anyone who could spend a whole day with thirty children should be applauded.

Some teachers resent social workers. Teachers refer children who have problems, who disrupt the class, who simply are not able to learn. Teachers want the social worker to produce some change.

After all, that is the social worker's job. Teachers are not impressed with elaborate testing, case records, diagnostic statements, jargon, or generalizations about behavior which they have heard a thousand times (Wadsworth, 1970). None of these have helped Johnny learn. In many cases the social workers cannot produce what the teachers want.

Between these extremes of opinion, Barbara often found herself dealing with a principal whose main attitude toward problem children was, "Suspend, suspend, suspend." In her own mind, Barbara worked out a middleground "systems approach" to her work long before concern with the system had become a vogue idea.

She described it in a paper she wrote for a conference of school social workers in 1965. "There is usually one thing that a child does that upsets the teacher. If I can deal with that one thing I can really affect the teacher. My determination is that every time I assist a teacher, I am assisting twenty-five children. This also helps in my relationship with the teachers.

"I find that first I must prove myself in a school. I do not tell people what I am going to do. I do it. There is a lot of skepticism about mental health workers in the school system. There is also a great deal of confusion about just what the school social worker does. I had a difficult time learning to say no. I had to say it in such a way as to insure that it did not sound like I did not care. The best technique was to say that I could do what was requested but that would mean some other part of the job could not be done. It was a matter of teaching the other personnel what I could and could not do."

Barbara received a great deal of praise from her colleagues and superiors for her speech. The events which followed surprised everyone and shocked the central administration in BCG. The speech served to catalyze workers in different regions. While different groups had different concerns, a common thread was the system —schools were not adapting to the needs of the children, reading scores were dropping, vandalism was increasing, and discipline in the classroom was becoming a major problem.

At first, the central administration did not know how to respond. Individual supervisors tried to explain why nothing could be done. Their responses varied: no money, not the right time given the atmosphere in the legislature, promises to bring the issues to the attention of higher ups, and agreement that it was terrible. Finally, the pressure was so strong that a total staff meeting at BCG was called.

BCG traditionally held an all-day staff meeting at the beginning and end of the school year. Agitation caused a change. A staff meeting was held on February 4, 1966. The administration was accused of doing nothing, paying lip service but not following through, distorting the actual situation in the schools, and blacklisting staff who expressed disagreement. The administrators responded that staff really did not know all the facts, that they were forced to follow Board of Education procedures themselves, and that they had to constantly fight against the other bureaus to maintain the program.

Barbara took a back seat at this meeting as it was clearly out of hand. Finally, when exhaustion was setting in she suggested that a joint committee of staff and administration meet to clarify just what the issues were. The staff held a hasty caucus at the conclusion of the meeting. Barbara and five militant social workers were chosen as the staff representatives. The administration would probably have agreed to anything in order that this meeting end.

A classic technique of administrations threatened with staff revolt is to simply not call staff meetings. Innumerable reasons are given. If pressed, the administration will simply say that meetings are not productive, they only lead to acrimony and poor morale.

Some administrations divide and conquer by soliciting recalcitrant staff members. BCG did this by designating certain schools as special schools. Each of the special schools was to have one full-time social worker. Sadly, this tactic often works. Those who seemed most adament about staging a coup suddenly begin a different type of cooing.

Resistance to Change

The function of confrontation is to state the issues starkly and strip away rationalizations and evasions. The intent is to force both parties to take some stand. Often one party forces the confrontation.

This tactic can lead to the resolution of difficulties and open up a continuing discussion over issues. On the other hand, clarifying issues can lead to more conflict. For the first time, one side senses the destructive capacity of the other.

Certain therapeutic psychologies emphasize the positive value of confrontation. However, this idea should not be carried over into the work situation where the relationships are not therapeutically oriented. At work, contending parties are seldom geared toward completely understanding and questioning their own motivations. Nor are formal staff meetings very helpful settings for clarifying such issues. In the past workers have been afraid of confrontations. Now, younger workers seem to relish them. Neither approach is helpful. This ultimately became clear at BCG.

The staff and administration planning group did not communicate better with one another than the total groups had done. Finally, one of Barbara's colleagues suggested that they probably would never get anywhere unless they understood each other better. This worker was involved in encounter groups. He suggested that outside experts in sensitivity training be brought in to set up a series of seminars to assist the group in resolving feelings and emotions which block effective problem-solving and decision-making (Birnbaum, 1969). The administration agreed to the suggestion, and a series of T groups were held in April.

Top administration of BCG did not attend the T groups. As a result, group resolutions were transmitted to the chiefs who had not benefited from the group meetings. The meetings focused more on interpersonal relationships than on substantive problems. It is all very well to understand that a teacher has a control problem. It is entirely another matter to understand the reasons a complex school system does not work and to map out a strategy for changing it.

Delay is also another inevitable result of T groups. They bring out hidden hostility which is not quickly resolved. There is much strain between maintaining honest and open interpersonal relationships and an organization's need to have things done efficiently and effectively.

People did come to understand each other in a different way than they had prior to the training sessions. Yet, the ardor of the staff was dampened. A subtle accommodation process had taken place. Staff recognized that supervisors have their problems too; and by acquiescing to the training groups, administration made it less likely that the lower level staff could act in concert as a pressure group.

Pressure campaigns depend upon emotions and simplifications of issues. Otherwise, the hesitancy to act overwhelms the desire to act. Some measure of depersonalization is required to bring about change on a broad scale.

After many months the administration joined the staff in formulating a general statement to the Board of Education urging local control of schools. While the BCG chiefs may have been sincere, it seemed more like, "If you can't beat them, join them." This approach channels hostility toward some other source. The Board of Education became the bad guys.

What power did BCG staff have to make their mild protest work? A few of the social workers quit, but most realized that quitting or going on strike would have very little effect. One of the more involved workers was well read in the theory and practice of social change. He brought an article for several of his friends to read.

> If a revolution harbors the illusion that a reign of terror will purify a bureaucracy of scoundrels and exploiters, it will fail. . . . It is the built-in forces of life in a bureaucracy that result in the bureaucracy being so indifferent to suffering and aspiration.
>
> Assuming power in a bureaucracy is controlled by a vast cadre of middle managers who are essentially homeostatic, and assuming the softness and purposelessness of the system in which they operate, it is conceivable that a critical mass of change agents working within that system may be effective in achieving increasingly significant ad hoc successes [Dumont, 1970, p. 14].

Bureaucratic guerrillas must not fear losing their jobs or embarrassing their superiors, must not be concerned simply with keeping the program alive and continually expanding its budget, must not set themselves the task of maintaining stable relationships with groups that have vital interests in the bureaucracy. The guerrillas must establish a network of communication and collaboration in order to frustrate the bureaucracy. They must constantly force the attention of the press, the public, and interest and professional groups toward anything that can embarrass and call the bureaucracy to task. Access to information is a major resource for guerrillas.

> *This network, in order to avoid the same traps of the bureaucracy it is meant to frustrate, should never become solidified or rigidified in structure and function. It may have the form of a floating crap game whose location and participation are fluid and changing, but whose purpose and activities are constant. The contacts should remain informal, nonhierarchical and caste oriented. . . . The makeup of each task force is an ad hoc, self-selected clustering of individuals whose skills or location or access to information suggests their roles. This network of change agents becomes a reference group, but not a brotherhood. There need not be a preoccupation with loyalty, cordiality, or steadfastness. They do not even have to be friendly [Dumont, 1970, p. 14].*

Is the terrain suitable for guerrilla warfare? Who will feed the guerrillas when they must hide? How can they deal with informers or with a blacklist? How can one bureaucratic guerrilla group be kept from frustrating the plans of another guerrilla group? It is fairly easy to defoliate a department.

Guerrilla warfare will probably lower whatever level of service is currently being offered. Peasants lose the most in guerrilla warfare because both sides attack them. In agencies, the clients lose.

Guerrilla warfare would not work in BCG without allies external to the schools. Guerrillas operating alone in a bureaucracy ultimately will be weeded out. Most staff are afraid of speaking up for fear of being designated troublemakers.

Strategy

The desire for local control was based on the assumption that local control would inevitably result in changes in the system, including more influence for BCG.

Barbara's view of the system was broader in scope. She

recognized that neither the higher nor lower staff at BCG should decide how mental health resources should be employed. This decision must be made in the context of the total school system. Conceivably such a decision could downgrade BCG.

A Do-Good Organizational Secret: Departments tend to define what is good for themselves as good for the organization. This is seldom true.

Barbara also recognized that there are difficulties with both centralized and decentralized school systems. While her colleagues saw community control as a panacea, she saw it as a useful mechanism for strengthening accountability.

Six months after the BCG staff statement was sent to the Board of Education, local control of schools became a reality. Agitation by a variety of public interest groups carried the day. Seven semi-autonomous boards were to be created. Members were to be appointed to these boards who were representative of the area's ethnic, social, and political groupings. As such they were similar to the boards of many social agencies.

Shifting from the initiation to the implementation stage of organization change is difficult. Techniques useful in getting an innovation initiated are considerably less useful in implementation.

Staff use all their energy to get an idea accepted and have none left to carry on the battle of implementation. They assume they have a plan when all they have is an unoperationalized intent. The confrontations, T-groups, and guerrilla warfare can simply wear out most of the staff.

Staff who were excellent leaders in the initiation struggle often do not have the ability to take the lead in implementation where a different type of knowledge and judgment is required. It is at this point where greatest caution must be exercised. Obstructionists know full well the value of giving them enough rope to hang themselves. Community control, for example, is full of traps.

When Donald Miller, principal of one of the schools Barbara was assigned to, told her of his plan for organizing a new community school board, Barbara made several points.

People can come to one meeting, miss two or three, and then come back for a few. Ultimately, control of community groups begins to rest in a small executive committee. Then people tend to vote more on personal contacts than on the substance of issues.

There is no way to organize a community board that is absolutely representative of the community. Even if a public election is held, elected officials are not easily held to account by the public. Open public meetings often degenerate into shouting matches, especially when there are sharp issues. Thus, there is very little open communication between the public and the board.

Even when community boards are appointed with representatives from every ethnic, class, and interest group, constituents have no way of holding them to account. Because they do not report back to any organized body, they tend to be free agents.

At local meetings people rise and say, "The community wants." They are really saying that they want and the community are those who have similar ideas to theirs. Each community is made up of many subgroups which have diverse and often conflicting interests. The best that one can do is to insure that any one faction of a community can be dislodged. Rules and regulations must be set up so that other factions have a possibility of gaining power.

Community groups seldom know how to carry out the tasks assigned to them. Some community groups have no idea how to make judgments concerning the abilities of one principal versus another. The most simplified criteria are used, often to the detriment of the school. Verbal facility and personal contact with influential people are seldom the best criteria.

Some community groups can confuse setting a policy with administering it. Some people in the community want to sit in on the classes and watch the teachers in order to report any mistakes. Once given power, the oppressed often becomes the oppressors.

Community control of local agencies in poor neighborhoods is often accompanied by hiring local poor people as case or teacher aides. These people, lacking credentials, are unable to move from one organization or job to another and are therefore insecure about their jobs.

These indigenous personnel often define themselves as the community. If incompetent, they are difficult to fire as they will organize their neighbors in protest. Agency executives are usually afraid of such protests as they threaten the image of the agency and potentially its source of funds. A board that is controlled by either its professional or its indigenous staff cannot function. If incompetent staff cannot be fired, there is little point in having a board or an executive director. There are additional complexities.

People participate in community groups for many reasons. Some enjoy participation. Others seek to meet clients for their business or profession, gain publicity, or fulfill some ideological or personal commitment.

Politically motivated participants are not so much interested in quality education as they are in gaining control of schools as a staging ground for political power. They assume that once they are in control they can create a social movement to unite all poor, low income communities in pressing for better and more adequate services. They are willing to have services decline in the short run to preserve their political base (incompetent personnel who are politically loyal would not be fired). Ultimately, segments of the community will not wish to have good service relegated to secondary priority, and conflict will result.

A basic mistake made in organizing community school boards or boards of directors of social agencies is the choice of the structure. The usual method is to choose the traditional structure: chairmen, vice-chairmen, and general membership divided into committees such as personnel, program, and finance.

There are monthly meetings of the membership plus committee meetings. An executive committee meets in between the general membership meetings. *Robert's Rules of Order* is the bible, and the organization runs according to traditional democratic procedures. Decisions are based on membership voting.

This structure is not suited for every situation. It tends to recruit the middle class, verbally sophisticated participant. It is better to choose a structure that is suited to the goals of the agency. The traditional structure with its formal meetings is not suited for communicating with large groups of people on an ongoing basis. Yet, this type of communication is vital if a school board is to be accountable to a community.

Since it is virtually impossible to get a board that is representative of the wishes of all segments of the community, it is best to keep large numbers of people aware of what the school is attempting to do and how well it is succeeding. Should disagreements arise, board changes can be made on the basis of knowledge and information (Weissman, 1970, pp. 167–178; Perlmutter, 1972).

This last point intrigued Mr. Miller. He asked Barbara, "Isn't there terrific pressure on my teachers as well as myself to doctor the statistics a little, to make it look as if we are doing better than we actually are? Even without lying, would it not be possible to construe certain situations as more positive than they are? Isn't the board completely dependent on what we tell them?"

He was quite correct. The only way to counter this is to put part of the responsibility for the evaluation onto the board itself. The board can ask parents whether their child has improved in reading, has had his problems in learning alleviated. The board can also speak with the children.

In this manner, professional evaluation can be checked with the personal evaluation of the family. Utilizing parents not on the board to survey other parents is an effective way of creating a large body of citizens knowledgeable about the school and able to judge the worth of a school board. Giving a board independent access to evaluative information would do more than anything else to erase the rubber stamp so commonly used for lack of knowledge or information.

If the problems are anticipated and it is clear beforehand what a board member has to do, a great many difficulties can be mitigated and a useful board can develop. Stating clearly that so many hours per month will be required can only have a salutary effect. Board members also require some training on how a school operates, how to think about success and failure, and how to frame judgments.

There is nothing that service organizations do that the average citizen cannot comprehend. If 90 percent of the clients of a psychiatric clinic say that they receive no substantial help through their contact with the clinic, then it matters little how involved or complex the therapeutic techniques utilized are. They are not working. Laymen may not know what to do, but they certainly know that something different should be done.

Board-training is an old idea in social agencies that has

never worked well. After they are trained, board members still do not have independent access to information about the agency. They remain forever dependent on the staff for information.

Mr. Miller's final question was more difficult. Would not such a board still get bogged down in policy disputes over bussing, quotas of teaching staff based on ethnicity, internal politicking based on status drives, animosity to certain staff members, and factionalism? In fact, would not access to more information create more disputes? Barbara answered that it might, but a focus on school achievement could put parameters on the disputes.

In a nearby city, experimental community school boards had been set up in poverty areas without guidelines for judging effectiveness of the schools. Without objectives, the interplay of representation from various groups—parents, community, teachers, and students—was dissipated in vague dialogues over racism and educational ideology.

The problems an active board presents must be weighed against the detriments of a passive board. Many executives prefer a passive board. An active board constrains their personal freedom of action and threatens their job security if matters do not go well.

Discussion

Boards of directors have three primary functions (Stein, 1962). They establish the right or legitimacy of the agency to carry on its program and sanction its activities. They are responsible for setting the overall policy of the agency, whether it is going to give individual charity, set up a job-training service, create recreation programs, or serve Catholics or Jews. Boards of private agencies are responsible for fund-raising.

While some public agencies have advisory committees, most do not have boards of directors. All private agencies have boards of varying size. Some boards meet regularly once a month; others have only an annual meeting. A board which meets once a year obviously does little in terms of setting policy or ensuring that the agency is doing what it says it is doing.

The high-powered board consists of young corporation executives and successful local businessmen. This board can raise money and get doors opened for the agency. It wants the agency to run efficiently, it does not want any trouble with complaining staff, and it does not want to be bothered with details. Unfortunately, some of the details are what is happening to the clients.

The agenda for board meetings are sent in advance along with considerable amounts of material to be read prior to the meeting. This appears to be a real board of directors; yet, it is all style and form, with little substance. A group of businessmen meeting once a month cannot really make decisions about whether a neighborhood needs a child care clinic or a job placement bureau.

A high-powered board generally hires a high-powered executive who knows how to keep the board happy and run the agency his own way. He gives the board just the right amount of the right information. The high-powered board is really a rubber stamp board.

The one man board is dominated by one person because he either gives a tremendous donation to the agency or works the hardest at getting money for the agency. This person is generally quite egocentric and is handled by the executive director with kid gloves. Unfortunately, this person generally has a very low view of staff. The agency belongs to him because he paid for it.

Some boards are dominated by a small clique called the executive committee. The board acquiesces to whatever the executive committee decides because friends of the executive committee have been briefed in advance.

Boards are not quasi-legislative bodies where the majority rules. Boards almost always establish a consensus. Generally, there are no opposition parties. Because the members are volunteers, those who constantly lose will soon drop out. The chairman of the board is generally elected unanimously. Because no one wants to lose an election, only one person is nominated by the nominating committee.

In most situations the board and the executive are hand in glove. The board hires the executive to take care of the agency. In so doing, the board relinquishes most of its responsibility. Almost all such boards of directors are a joke. This is a tragedy for them and their agencies.

In most agencies, beginning level social workers have little or no contact with the board. Thus, there is little possibility and no legitimacy for such a worker to ask questions about board functioning.

One way for a worker to raise the issue so that the agency must seriously debate it is to use the local chapter of the National Association of Social Workers. Organize a committee on board-agency functioning. Rather than argue the question of which interests should be represented on a board, focus on board procedures.

One such committee issued a report which included this revolutionary statement: "It is the responsibility of the board to develop an independent assessment of an agency's functioning. Boards must have procedures for rotating members on and off. Board members should have opportunities for observing programs and talking with clients, providing clients agree."

Reports like this can make it possible for workers in many agencies to raise issues. Surprisingly, support may come from the board. Most board members are bored with being rubber stamps and would welcome a means of becoming less dependent.

A report such as this can also help staff relate more easily with the board. It can sanction ongoing discussion between the two. Staff workers generally have little access to the board. There is, nevertheless, often a formal procedure by which staff can petition to bring matters to the attention of the board. This is seldom used for a variety of reasons: the time and effort required to negotiate this formal procedure through the administrative hierarchy; disagreements among staff themselves; tendency of boards to accept the executive's views; and fears of retaliation.

A context for discussion must be set up. A board which only knows what the executive tells it is not going to be of much use to a staff, especially a staff whom the board has never seen or talked with outside of a crisis.

An information-giving process should be ongoing and is best instituted in noncrisis situations where resistance from top administration is likely to be minimal. Every third board meeting, for example, could be turned into a board-staff seminar. The information transmitted should not be about the administration, but about the social problems with which the agency contends.

Boards are a difficult challenge. Without them it is unlikely that there can be real accountability. With them, there is potential for conflict, stalemate, and delay. In addition, professionals seek freedom of action. Will intelligent, trained personnel who have spent three months planning a program really let laymen call it into serious question?

A state of tension must be sought where staff and board force each other to the limits of capacity without creating immobilization. Boards have the right to determine what should be accomplished, but not the right to determine how it is to be accomplished. Populism and professionalism work best when there is tension between the two.

Barbara's colleagues assumed that once boards were set up, such problems as overloaded caseloads, insufficient staff, and administrative unresponsiveness would be overcome. They did not know, however, how boards would achieve this. The complexities of community groups, board structure, job insecurities, and political interests were beyond them. An inability to operationalize a plan can be disastrous.

Quotes from Dumont's "Down the Bureaucracy," published by permission of Transaction, Inc. from *Transaction,* vol. 7, October 1970. Copyright © 1970 by Transaction, Inc.

6

Utilizing
Organizational
Tension

Subtle and complex, the structure of an organization has the in-
finitely difficult task of withstanding tension. It must deal with
three distinct yet interrelated sources of tension. There are tensions
derived from the desires of staff for status, promotion, and security
that conflict with organizational ends. There are tensions derived
from the internal operation of the organization—conflicting roles,
procedures, perceptions, goals, and interests. And there are tensions
derived from the external relations of the organization—conflicts
caused by the simultaneous desire to raise money, maintain legitimacy, insure survival, gain the cooperation of related organizations,
and be successful.

Such tensions are felt by individuals in their organizational

76

roles as they carry out their work. A key function of an agency's arrangement of roles and processes is to handle tension. If there were no tension, there would be little need for an administrative hierarchy. How tension is handled and whether it promotes agency effectiveness is the topic of this chapter.

A Do-Good Organizational Secret: Tensions are inevitable in organizations. The way they are handled is not.

Adjustments in caseload, staff qualifications, intake policy, and training are all ways of handling tension. When any method results in and maintains poor service to clients, it must become the target of change. One way such methods can be changed is by simultaneously suggesting new ways of tension management and making it increasingly undesirable to maintain the old way by creating new tensions related to it.

Scope of the Problem

Bill Johnson has worked for many years in public welfare. He is black and grew up in Harlem. His father insisted that he learn a trade. By the time Bill was twenty-five, he had decided not to spend his life in a furniture factory. It took him six years of night school to finish college. Shortly after graduation, he applied to the welfare department because he liked working with people.

Bill has done quite well in the department. After only four years, he received an educational leave to go to Columbia University for his master's degree in social work. Now he supervises five caseworkers, all with B.A. degrees.

A majority of the public seem to feel that a public assistance agency is a bank which accepts no deposits, only withdrawals. Certainly, then, the Public Assistance Department of Met City is a funny looking bank. It has as many branch offices as Chase Manhattan, but its offices are dull and dingy and filled with noisy people and unsmiling clerks. It has more customers than Chase Manhattan, but Chase is not worried.

The Triboro branch is housed on the fourth and fifth floors of a large factory building. The first three floors contain a variety of small manufacturing concerns. The fourth floor is approximately three hundred feet long and one hundred and twenty-five feet wide.

It holds three hundred desks, in rows of thirty and columns of ten. Somewhere near the fifty yard line, Bill Johnson has his desk. Some days he just sits there and dreams that he is back on his high school football team plowing right through all those desks, stumbling into the end zone (which, in the Triboro center, houses the supervisors' offices).

In Met City, the department operates out of six local centers similar to Triboro. Each of the centers has the same staffing pattern: a director, an assistant director, an administrative assistant, and senior case supervisors who supervise five case supervisors who supervise five to eight supervisors who each supervise five caseworkers.

Morale in the department has deteriorated rapidly in the last several years. Bill and his friends feel that they are merely connections in a computer that has a self-defeating mechanism. No matter what they do, the results are always the same.

School confirmed one of Bill's previous judgments. People's lives are too varied and complex to be encompassed by any one policy or procedure manual. While it may seem logical to require authorization of a case supervisor for the payment of rent above a particular level, when there is a shortage of housing and a deposit must be placed immediately or the housing will be lost, such policies and procedures are dysfunctional. It may seem rational that money allotted for the payment of a gas bill be used for that purpose. After all, without gas there will be no heat, possible illness, strain, and stress. On the other hand, when the grants are skimpy it is also rational for a mother to take a little of this allotment to give spending money to her children so that they do not join those on the street who steal.

Because the department does not have its own funds, it can provide only those services for which the state and federal governments are willing to reimburse the department. Very few municipalities are able to afford the cost on their own. A family may need nursing services, but none is available if the services are not reimbursable. It is like the old Ford slogan, the customer can have any color car he wants as long as it's black. Funding rather than client need dictates the availability of services.

The director at Triboro, Mr. Lemmel, worked his way up

through the department, starting as a caseworker in the middle 1940s. He believes in following the procedures and policies. Unfortunately for those who work under him, he is not willing to assume responsibility. Because of this, a variety of dysfunctional ways of handling tension have developed.

Lemmel is invariably called downtown or has someone ill in his family on the days when new policies are to be implemented. Without someone who can make decisions, confusion reigns at the center. There is no leadership because the high administrative positions are filled with Lemmel's cronies.

Line workers need specific case interpretations of policy. In addition, they need someone to listen to what they have to say about the advisability of particular policies and procedures. The central office policy makers failed to translate the ramifications of their policies and procedures into the time necessary for line workers to carry them out. Any policy or procedure might make a great deal of sense individually, but when added to all the other policies and procedures that workers have to implement it may become sheer idiocy.

The symbol of this idiocy is the insistence on keeping accurate statistics. Line workers must note the number of home visits made, the number of contacts with institutions, and the exact type of service performed for the client. To the central office, these statistics are extremely important. They are the means by which the agency is reimbursed for its services. To the line workers, the statistics are neither actual nor factual. The department has to get a certain level of reimbursement to function; therefore, the statistics show that level of service. As one worker put it, "If no one does anything the system will go on." A more perceptive worker said, "Statistics never tell the whole truth. They may note the number of visits made, but they tell nothing of the number not made."

At the Triboro Center, frustration and unhappiness are more the rule than the exception. Ultimately, the clients bear the brunt of the situation. Without high morale, the job of a welfare worker is almost impossible to do. "To get a person a check, you have to run up the goddamn stairs four or five times. After a while you just get worn down. You are dealing with staff who do not seem to care. With all the paper work and the resistance to changing anything, you end up only worrying about your survival. Nothing else makes sense. The whole time you feel bad, then you stop feeling. You actually do not have to work. All you have to do is show that you are doing work."

Resistance to Change

What can be done about a department which is accountable to no one? Public mistrust, staff defensiveness and weariness, and client hostility and apathy have all combined to produce a system that runs like a scared rabbit—darting and dashing from one point to another, stopping only long enough to shiver.

When he first came to the department, Bill followed the rules meticulously. When he needed exceptions to particular procedures, he prepared his case, clearly articulating the need for exception. These requests were then forwarded to the central office for careful screening. The commissioner felt that too much discretion at the local level would create chaos in the organization.

The central bureau people that handled exceptions were aware that exceptions granted freely could become precedents, and they would lose control. They scrutinized each case, sending it back with questions not directly related to the exception. For example, Bill requested an exception on a rent level and was asked for verification of the divorce of Mrs. Gonzalez from Pedro Gonzalez. The marriage was common-law and had taken place in Puerto Rico. It was unlikely that verification could be secured, and if it could it would take months.

Bill quickly stopped asking for exceptions. He started to look for other ways to get clients the extra money they needed. For example, there are allowances for special grants. If someone is ill in the family or a telephone is necessary for emergencies, a telephone can be secured. A request for the telephone is written out, even though there is no medical emergency. The additional money secured for the telephone can be used to pay the additional rent.

The issue is quite simple. Supervisors do not wish to pass upon exceptions which they have no authority to authorize. If the case is passed up to the higher level, they might be asked to fill out more forms and receive back questions that would require a great deal of work to answer. A kind of bargaining develops: allow me this grant for which you have authority, and I will not bother asking for this other thing.

This bargaining arrangement is more implicit than explicit. Trading creates a situation where everyone is hiding something. Everyone has something to be afraid of. Few are then willing to take the risks involved in bringing about change.

As the clients became organized in the late 1960s, they campaigned to have every case brought up to standard. Every client was to get every special allowance entitled to him. This, along with the increasing numbers of people enrolled, caused the state legislature to do away with special grants. There were now only flat grants. Thus a great deal of discretion that the workers once had to use in favor of the clients was done away with. Nevertheless, the tactic was not without drawbacks. Not every worker was willing to take the time and effort to fight the matter for the client.

There are always a number of people who want to make an agency work better. These people inevitably find themselves on staff advisory committees. Bill was one of these. Lemmel did not actually refuse to meet with the staff advisory committee; he simply asked the assistant director to go in his place.

It soon became obvious that approval had to be asked from the central office for any issue of substance. Somehow this approval could never be secured. Along the chain of communication, something would happen. One could seldom find out where or why.

This situation is most infuriating; so is the delay. Ultimately, the staff planning committee can do something about fire drills, but not much else unless the director is interested in promoting changes. Lemmel was not. He used delay.

Clearly, Lemmel was a major stumbling block to change. Even if information about his incompetence could be communicated to the higher administrative levels, it is doubtful that anything would be done. Without a board which holds the agency accountable, information from lower level staff about higher level staff tends to be ignored. Civil service, personal ties, and indifference combine to defeat what seems rationally desirable.

A major problem is the size and centralization of the welfare department. For the line worker, the department is simply too enormous to get to the people who make decisions. Bill is insulated from the policy makers by seven layers of bureaucracy.

Reorganization is needed. Probably 95 percent of all exceptions could be decided by second level administration. At Triboro this is the caseworker's supervisor's supervisor, the case supervisor. With authority so located, a collegial atmosphere among work groups of five or six staff and one supervisor might be created, thereby raising the quality of work and morale without lessening accountability. The present atmosphere leads to buck-passing and collusion. Nevertheless, the issue for Bill was not so much what was the best method of reorganization but how could he influence Triboro to begin moving toward more local autonomy.

Strategy

Although Lemmel was not a director who wanted authority, increasing the discretionary power of the directors of the local centers was important. Then, at least, there would be a lever that workers could potentially reach. There are a number of ways this problem could be approached. Some of the directors undoubtedly want more authority. Staff can help them get it.

How does a line worker like Bill locate such directors and assist them? First, the agency underground knows a lot about the people. Second, seemingly innocuous ad hoc groups—such as Concerned MSWs for the Welfare Department—can be helpful. On the surface, these groups have bland professional and educational goals such as discussing behavior therapy. Actually, they have the potential for dealing with more controversial matters.

It is extremely difficult to organize staff. Differences in interests, fear of reprisal, lack of commitment, and a host of other factors combine to defeat such efforts. Concerned MSWs took a long time to organize. Six or seven dedicated members were intelligent enough to develop a number of rewards for participating, from social affairs, to opportunities to meet and be known by those outside of one's center, to opportunities to know others who could grant favors.

In addition, the organization did not begin by presenting the administration with a series of demands or by electing a president.

Bill realized that he would make a very poor president in terms of his ability to attract people in positions of authority to the organization. He and his friends waited until they could interest a very intelligent director of another center in the job.

In the first year, meetings had topics like "Curriculum in the Schools of Social Work and the Welfare Department." Resistance, fears, and suspicions were thus diluted until the organization could develop strength and decide how best to proceed in bringing about change.

Ultimately, Concerned MSWs began agitating for more local discretion and for advisory boards to the local centers. Yet, one organization can seldom accomplish all of its goals because some goals or procedures conflict. Concerned MSWs could not blow the whistle on Lemmel and other incompetents like him if the organization was seeking their cooperation for some other project. Bill saw that in such situations two organizations have to be formed. He also realized that once an organization reaches its objective, keeping the organization alive may no longer be useful.

When Bill returned from school, he and several of his friends organized a workers' union. It had the assistance of the local branch of the city and office employees' union staff. A big selling point to the membership was that it would give them job security, bargaining power for salary raises, and an organized voice in dealing with management over professional issues such as caseload, working conditions, and treatment of clients.

The union has turned out to be a mixed blessing (Goldberg, 1960). While it has been useful in gaining higher salaries, it has, along with civil service, made it almost impossible for the administration to get rid of incompetent workers. The union takes an advocacy stand in favor of its members. It is forced to pull out every stop before a member can be fired. This brings about a type of bargaining between management and union where incompetent workers are merely transferred. They become someone else's problem in the organization. Management eventually gives up trying to get rid of incompetent workers. It accepts lower standards of performance, and ultimately the total performance of the agency is corroded.

To Bill's dismay, he found that the union was really unable

to deal with professional issues. The union had to include both the
service workers and the clerical and maintenance workers. Whenever negotiations were going on, nonservice workers were mainly
interested in salary. Once salary issues were settled, they were not
interested in holding out for lower case loads or better facilities and
services for the clients. They had full voting rights within the
union. Two separate unions would have created too much dissension
within the organization. By virtue of its involvement in personnel
grievances, the union pushed its officers to consider mainly salary
and working conditions. Someone described the union as the oppressed becoming the oppressor. Union members were willing to
trade client benefits for their own ends in bargaining with administration.

In addition, Bill found that the power to strike was not very
much power. No one but the clients seemed to be terrifically in-
convenienced when the workers struck. Once automation of checks
was instituted throughout the system, even they were not incon-
venienced a great deal. Unionism turned out to be useful as a check
to an arbitrary administration, but not a solution for problems of
inefficient and ineffective administration.

The real value of the union was latent. The union made it
possible for many workers who might otherwise have been afraid, to
speak out at staff meetings and join Concerned MSWs. The union
provided the backbone for agitation for more accountability and
more discretion at the local level.

The difference between manifest and latent functions of
organizations is a useful distinction for planning strategies of change.
The latent function of both the union and Concerned M.S.W.s turned
out to be quite important. The manifest function of one other type
of organization proved useful.

Welfare client groups sprang up all over the country during
the middle 1960s. Bill knew some of the leaders of these groups in
Met City. He suggested that they bring a court suit against the
department for unreasonable delay in making dispositions of applications. This suit was won. The court ordered that public aid
applications be disposed of in thirty days (Lindsey, 1973).

The use of the courts is an important tool for staff. The

court-ordered speedup made the department's high command seriously think about the necessity of granting more discretion to local centers. Agencies do not like to be taken to court; it is time-consuming, costly, and potentially damaging to their public image.

In his strategy to create more local autonomy, Bill utilized a fifth organization, the local chapter of the National Association of Social Workers. The emphasis of NASW traditionally has been on the individual worker and his personal professional accountability. NASW saw its role as providing assurance to the public that its members possessed certain skills and adhered to a specific code of ethics.

Bill organized a subcommittee on welfare in his local chapter. This subcommittee argued that since the agency is a major intervening variable between the worker and his ability to effectively help his clients, NASW must also be concerned with agencies. Ultimately, the chapter took a stand for more local discretion in welfare centers. They also came out for local advisory boards composed of representatives of citizen groups, clients, staff, and public officials.

The orchestration of the union, courts, Concerned MSWs, politicians, client groups, and the professional association effected a change in the discretion granted local centers and also aided in Lemmel's early retirement. A new set of consequences had been created. Organizational tensions could no longer be handled in the same old fashion.

Such an orchestration is not possible with more controversial issues such as the benefit levels paid to recipients. Public controversy blocks change. In such cases, the line worker must develop a long-term political strategy (Weissman, 1972).

Public attitudes concerning the work ethic, eligibility requirements, minimum wage laws, job-training, and employment programs influence the operation of public welfare departments. It can be argued that there is little value in trying to make existing departments work more effectively for the client, given the inadequacy of most benefit levels and the unavailability of services.

There are, of course, a variety of current proposals such as the negative income tax, guaranteed income, and children's allowances which would offer an alternative to public welfare. However, it is unlikely that the public welfare program will be done away within the near future.

Bill Johnson concluded that the present welfare system is a stopgap measure until other solutions are found. To achieve anything, he realized that he had to make a long-term commitment to stay in welfare, and that he would have to stick his neck out. In addition, he knew that a great deal had to be done outside of the organization. He had to be active politically, and he had to promote better public understanding of the problems of the welfare client and of the alternative means by which poverty can be dealt with in the country.

Discussion

There is tension between what clients want and what agencies can offer. Delay was one of the ways in which the welfare department managed this tension. Bill Johnson succeeded in negating this technique by creating a whole new set of tensions which made it undesirable for the department to continue utilizing delay in disposition of cases.

At the same time, he forced the department to consider different methods of dealing with such tensions by their acceptance of more local autonomy. Presumably they could have hired more staff at central headquarters to process requests. His basic strategy is worth remembering: Before one attempts to change the way agencies handle tension, one must have an alternative and a plan for making the agency adopt that alternative. These plans and alternatives must be clearly thought out, as it is all too easy for welfare systems to respond to increased tensions by cutting the rolls or lowering the benefits.

To win such struggles, workers must have a clear view of just what the sources of tension are in an organization and in its external relationships and how they are interconnected. Money and status are excellent starting points of analysis. In most agencies, there are a variety of departments or subunits. Conflict between departments can retard any effort to change agency arrangements.

A Do-Good Organizational Secret: The best kept secret of

social agencies is that policies ostensibly designed to promote the interests of clients also promote the interests of certain departments and individuals.

When there is potential for conflict and there is no conflict, it is important to know why. Informal relations, coalitions, and bargaining are often the order of the day. The best ideas often cannot be instituted in an agency because they may break up long-standing ways in which tensions are resolved. If such tensions cannot be removed, new ways of handling the tensions must be devised while old ways are rendered ineffective, if there is to be any change.

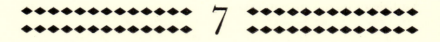
Lowering the Caseload

Competition and conflict among and between nonprofit organizations is as deadly as between any competing businesses (Reid, 1964). Fears and tension over loss of revenue, jealousies over prestige, and differences in ideology are difficult to resolve.

Social agencies do not operate in a vacuum. They have relationships with other social agencies—the settlement house with the school, the clinic with the hospital. The system in which a social agency operates is extremely important to its efforts. There is no point in a psychiatric unit improving its effectiveness in doing diagnostic workups on clients if there are no resources in the community where the clients can get the treatment that they require.

Workers at the lower rungs of agencies seldom visualize the necessity or possibility of their affecting agencies other than their own. Yet, many problems cannot be solved solely in the confines of an agency. The overextended caseload is a case in point.

88

Scope of Problem

For as long as Allison Tallnow could remember, she had always loved children. In high school, she decided to become a child welfare worker. The Stern-Longley Agency in Mountain City should have been an ideal place for her to work. It was not.

Stern-Longley traces its history back to the middle nineteenth century. Samuel Stern took Horace Greeley's advice and went West to make his fortune. He found his fortune and Mary Longley, a lady of no mean ambition. Myth has it that they met in a saloon— Mary at the head of a group of crusading women, and Sam at the head of the bar. It is definitely known that Sam began a clothing store which ultimately became the largest in the West, and Mary used the profits to support a variety of social causes from Bible-reading to playground-building. The Stern-Longley Agency bears their surnames. Mary founded it in 1882 and acted as its director until her death in 1907.

Over the years, a great many changes have taken place. Today the Stern-Longley Foundation supplies only 15 percent of the budget for the agency. The remainder comes from the city which pays the agency a fixed amount for each child to which it provides service. The board consists mainly of elderly women from socially prominent families, with a few men who serve because of their legal and financial expertise. The present director has made an effort to recruit younger board members.

The agency is housed in two large floors of a modern sky-scraper. The waiting room is filled with portraits of babies and young children. The appointments are modern and the walls are painted in bright colored pastels.

One floor houses the adoption department and the other, the foster care department. The foster care department is considerably larger. It includes three supervisors, fifteen caseworkers and five case aides. It is headed by an assistant director who reports directly to the executive director. The agency is quite professionalized. The administration, the supervisory staff, and over half of the caseworkers have their M.S.W.s. Psychiatric consultation is available to the staff for cases with a psychiatric aspect.

The director of the agency is Marietta Starr, one of the first professionally trained social workers in Mountain City and a member of a socially prominent family. Ms. Starr helped organize the first chapter of the National Association of Social Workers and has something of a national reputation in her field. She is highly intelligent, but somewhat foreboding.

Most of the staff, including Allison's supervisor, Ms. Melkin, are afraid to approach Ms. Starr. As a result, communication is lessened. It makes little sense to discuss issues at meetings when one's supervisor is unable to present those issues in a forceful and clear manner to the administration. Although the working conditions and salary at the agency were quite good, nothing else was right for Allison.

The agency espouses goals which it is never able to achieve. In essence, the agency acts as a surrogate parent for a child who is separated for some reason from his natural parents. This involves continuing concern for the child; finding, advising, and guiding foster parents; and attempting to assist and aid the natural parents in resuming their roles with their children. This can also involve helping the natural parents remain away from the child when such an association is deemed to be harmful to a child. The job of mediating and balancing the interests of the three parties is further complicated by the difficulties each of the parties may face.

Allison's field placement during her second year of graduate school was in a child welfare agency. Here she had a very carefully screened caseload of five families. The problems were quite delimited and specific—a mother who needed job-training, an alcoholic father, and a foster mother who tended to be punitive in her handling of children. Allison was able to visit each of the foster families at least once a month and saw several of the natural parents on a weekly basis.

The unreality of Allison's school experience became apparent soon after she joined Stern-Longley. She was informed that her caseload would average between twenty and thirty children. When the two natural parents and the two foster parents for each child were added, Allison knew she was out of school. There are, of course, good reasons for this situation. Someone has to take care of

the children, and the agency is reimbursed in terms of the number
of children it places.

In theory, the child's needs and problems are to be matched
with the capacity and capability of the foster parents and their
home. In fact, there existed a chronic shortage of foster homes in
Mountain City. Therefore, appropriate matching of a child to a
particular home rarely occurred.

An even sadder situation confronted Allison shortly after
she began her job. Several of her foster homes were not really fit
places for children. Yet, if she recommended that they be closed
down, there would be no place for the children to go. She quickly
learned to modify her expectations. A percentage of people who
maintained foster homes were in it simply for the money. An older
worker told Allison, "I do not begrudge them the money, considering what they often have to put up with." She also discovered
another dynamic caused by the chronic shortage of foster homes.
The more disorganized foster homes got the more disorganized
children. Better foster homes would not have them. Thus, a system
of "dumping homes" developed.

Allison spent most of her time firefighting. An endless round
of emergencies diverted her from any regular schedule of casework
interviews. These emergencies ranged from a child being expelled
from school, to a foster family refusing to keep a child, to the
natural parents wanting a child back, to foster parents not receiving
their monthly allotment, to court appearances. Caseworkers had to
learn to manage their caseloads. Emergencies came first; if time
was left, problems that were brewing came next. These problems
often were not worked out until they became emergencies. The bulk
of the caseload was simply forgotten because they never complained
or had no emergencies.

The natural parents tend to get lost in this hectic pace.
There is simply no time or resources left to deal with the problems
of the natural parents. What was to be a temporary situation evolves
into a semipermanent and often permanent situation.

In addition to the cost of the foster home, there is the cost
of a variety of other services. Psychiatric services, homemaker services, day care centers, and visiting nurses are rarely available

because of insufficient funds. Allotments paid by ADC are pitifully low in many states. When there are services, they simply are not accessible at the time when they are required. In many cases, had the services been available, the family would not have broken up in the first place.

Attending to emergencies and securing needed services wears the workers down. Allison had a difficult time gaining the cooperation of Mountain City's hospitals, schools, and social agencies. They were not willing to relax their rules and regulations sufficiently to take into account the personal needs of the children.

The agency did not evaluate the workers in terms of what was happening to the children. A good worker was someone who managed his caseload well, did not get ruffled by emergencies, and especially did not bring a great many problems to his supervisor. An older worker whom Allison admired told her, "It staggers the imagination to make judgments about the natural family, the child, and the community. Even if you make good judgments, no one knows. This whole hectic environment makes it possible for the field to keep a lot of incompetents. The emphasis on reporting and supervision really keeps us from looking at what we are accomplishing. The agency has never come to grips with the admittedly difficult problem of defining what it hopes to achieve."

Resistance to Change

Allison's first attempt to deal with the caseload problem occurred one afternoon when she happened to ride up on the elevator with Ms. Starr. She mentioned that she was pleased to meet her because she had been wanting to suggest that the total staff have some discussion about caseload. Ms. Starr said that she would be glad to do that, and asked Allison to prepare a memo for her documenting the facts of the case.

Allison gathered her data quickly and rushed off the memo to Ms. Starr. Three weeks passed and there was no response. Ms. Starr may have had more important things to do than immediately respond to the memo. Allison was aware of this, but as the weeks passed, she wondered what she should do. She finally sent another memo in which she mentioned that she and several of her colleagues had gathered additional information about the problems of the caseload and wondered whether staff time might be set aside for a discussion.

By this time, Allison had interested several of the other younger workers in the issue. They began mentioning it at their unit staff meetings. This agitation ultimately did bear fruit, though bitter fruit it was to be. A memo finally came around announcing a special staff meeting on December 15, a month hence, to discuss the caseload situation.

The salami game is one of the oldest in social agencies. It is carried out in exactly the same manner in sectarian, nonsectarian, public, or private agencies. The staff is angry and upset. A staff meeting is called in which the executive director listens to complaints: the caseload is too large and we are not able to provide good service. The executive director responds: money is in short supply; she knows how hard people are working; look what will happen to the children if the caseload is cut.

There is a lull in the meeting. Suddenly, Allison or her counterpart gives an impassioned speech stating that if it is not cut, look what will happen to the children. The executive director agrees that something must be done. It will have to be discussed with the board. If the heads of the units agree, a suggestion will be made that the caseload this fall not rise above twenty children per worker unless there is some catastrophe in the city. What is not said but implied is that the workers must maintain their present caseload. Allison is not yet ready to turn the children back to the city, put them in jail, or create a public scandal.

It takes from six months to a year for normal attrition to significantly reduce caseloads. By that time, some of the leaders in the movement to reduce the caseload have either left or are preparing to leave the agency, new workers have come in, and there is a city-wide emergency brewing in child care.

At Stern-Longley, the caseloads went below twenty in May. By September they were rising again. The staff protest movement had gotten a little of what it wanted. It got a little slice off the end of the salami. That little bit of salami got the administration off the hook and put the staff on it. Ms. Starr was an intelligent woman. She knew the problems with the caseloads. If she could have secured more staff to lighten the caseload, she would have.

Use of the salami game was not cynical; it was merely a matter of doing the best she could in a very difficult situation. She had also been at the agency long enough to know that she had not heard the last from Allison.

By March, Allison had not yet caught on to the salami game and thought that she had really made a dent in the caseload problem. She decided to zero in on the frustrations created by the innumerable emergencies. Firefighting took 40 to 45 percent of her time. New and different arrangements were needed so that more time could be spent working with the natural parents. The same process was repeated—memos, staff meeting—but with a different outcome. Ms. Starr had long been concerned with this problem and had periodically made reports on the subject to the board of directors. The board met the following week. They recommended that a prestigious management consulting firm, Croft-Watershed, be hired to make a study of the problem.

In October, Croft-Watershed consultants descended on the agency. They had a well-developed system for making social agencies more efficient. Nothing they heard from the supervisors or from the workers altered their opinion about the effectiveness of their system. It involved a different type of record keeping; and it emphasized the use of the telephone for making referrals and handling problems. The fact that many of the clients did not have telephones, and that personal contacts, observations, and interactions were a crucial part of the work did not seem to penetrate.

The final report was beautifully printed and bound. Each of the board members received a copy, as did the supervisors. It was discussed by the board in late February. The implication was that Ms. Starr would see to its implementation. No one ever mentioned it at the agency after March 1. Allison and her friends were completely demoralized. Some consulting firms are the modern day equivalent of the traveling medicine show. Not surprisingly, they find that every organization they advise needs just what is in their package, whether it be a better data processing system, linear programming, human relations programs, operations research, or snake oil.

Strategy

Allison left the agency in early fall to have children of her own. Unfortunately, she has no plans to return to child welfare work. If she were to return, she might try some different tactics.

A mess in a social agency is seldom made by one person and seldom cleaned up by one. A mess in a whole field such as child welfare is certainly not made by one agency. Most of the problems at Stern-Longley were problems in the provision of child welfare services in Mountain City and the state.

Knowing where a problem can be solved is a vital first step. How soluble is the caseload problem at Stern-Longley? If Stern-Longley decreases its caseload, some other agency will probably increase theirs. Just because problems are not solvable within an agency does not mean that the worker must simply acquiesce. It means that he must use a different set of tactical options. Focusing solely on the agency will bring only remorse and early retirement.

Most workers face problems that cannot wait until the composition of the board is changed or cooperation is secured from other agencies. A long-range goal could be to have all Mountain City public and private foster care agencies involve themselves in a total reappraisal of the system. In the meantime, a short-range goal is required. Stern-Longley should develop new policies and procedures that will make it easier for workers to handle the firefighting part of their job. Otherwise, the work is too frustrating, and staff morale and efficiency drop. Whatever one does to achieve either goal should not jeopardize the potential achievement of the other. Because there are innumerable ways to do any one thing, this concept helps rule out some of the alternative approaches.

Many supervisors let you do what you want as long as they do not officially know about it. Most of Allison's foster families were on the west side of Mountain City. Through her work she became friendly with the director of a west side settlement. He allowed her the use of his empty rooms in the morning to meet with groups of clients or one of the children. She found that she handled emergencies quicker if she spent time at the settlement; and, her clients were more likely to come to see her there than in her downtown office.

Once a worker is confident of the value of a particular course of action, then he can tell his supervisor, and some private documentation of the change can be made. "I have noticed that I spend more and more time at the settlement and actually save a terrific amount of time. Perhaps I should try to document this for you." Of course, other workers in the same situation could be of great help.

When this information is made public, the agency does not necessarily respond appropriately. The worker must anticipate who will raise what objections. At Stern-Longley, the greatest potential for objections and difficulty lies with Ms. Starr. In general, the more one knows about an executive director and his predecessor, the more one knows about the organization. Why did the last executive director leave? Where did he go? Where would the present director go? Some executive directors are hired to save money, others to get money. Knowledge about this can be useful as a source of influence.

Dealing with the boss is an intricate art. Seeing him as simply an obstructionist leads to adopting tactics that discount the director's need to maintain his own self-esteem, to take a long-range view of the agency, and to maintain a coherent authority structure.

Jay (1969, pp. 177–178) has suggested that dealing with the boss—who can block one's proposals, reject one's ideas, and frustrate one's plans—is a lot like meeting a lion in the jungle. If one turns and runs, the lion will chase by instinct; if one moves toward the lion and corners it, it will leap at one's throat out of fear.

One should advance steadily and confidently, making sure to leave a way out, a line of retreat. However bitter the row, a worker must always leave a way open for the supervisor to consent without backing down. The worker must keep back a significant fact, an alternative proposal, or a reasonable modification until his superior realizes the strength of the worker's determination. When the lion starts to look around for a way to retreat, a path is opened for him.

Stalking the lion is often played in conjunction with getting a commitment to a course of action before a specific type of action is a reality. For example, Allison might have maneuvered Ms. Starr into a series of training sessions on the effect of the community and community agencies on child welfare services. After the concept of the staff cooperating with workers and institutions in local neighborhoods is accepted, it becomes considerably harder six months later to discount the importance of the workers actually spending two or three days in the neighborhood.

Money spent on foster care services might more appropriately be put into services to prevent family breakup. Small group homes, or even large residential centers, might be more appropriate for some children than foster care. Perhaps the public should not purchase services from private agencies. It is unlikely that the child welfare agencies, public or private, will face these dilemmas on their own. There are simply too many conflicting interests. An outside force is required to deal with problems that cut across agencies.

The professional association and the media are two outside forces with which to create pressure. However, when newspapers and television are sensationalist, episodic, and exposé oriented, they force agencies into defensive postures.

There is a variety of ways of contacting the media. Generally there is one reporter for a newspaper or television news program who covers social welfare. Opportunities should never be missed to contact the media. Informal contacts can be helpful.

At times when individuals do not wish to risk themselves, representatives of a union, client organization, or a single client can make contact with those who assign as well as cover stories by simply calling them.

The best media campaign is one that articulates the problems with a service and suggests that the agencies come up with answers at a future date. Such a campaign is best begun a few months prior to the United Fund campaign to communicate the seriousness of its intent. A follow-up is done a month before the campaign starts.

A media campaign in Mountain City should be used to force all the agencies in the field to look at the total child welfare service system. No other type of evaluation makes sense. No one agency can really have an impact on a social problem. There is little value in reducing caseloads in one agency if another already overloaded agency must take up the slack.

A Do-Good Organizational Secret: Evaluation of individual agencies as entities shifts the focus of evaluation from the impact of agencies on social problems to their impact on individuals.

An NASW subcommittee on child welfare can be of help. It will never attack a local agency (directors and administrators of these agencies are also members of NASW and may be sitting on the committee), but it can clarify the dimensions of agency and system evaluations.

Like many agencies, Stern-Longley knew little about its own operation or what the other agencies in the child welfare field were doing. Agencies must systematically gather and utilize the following information.

Foster care is an extremely expensive program. Knowing why children are placed can suggest alternative programs. Stern-Longley and the other foster care agencies should know if children were placed because of the mental illness of one of the parents, child neglect or abuse, poor physical health of one of the parents, inability or unwillingness of the parent(s) to continue care for reasons other than mental illness, abandonment of the family, a severe mental problem affecting the well-being of the children, or the deviant and unmanageable behavior of a child (Wasserman, 1970, p. 95).

Agencies are often criticized in terms of who their clients are. Demographic data on children in foster care, data on the total number of children in the community, and data on the number of children who need foster care is required to intelligently discuss this criticism.

Effectiveness can be measured by what happens to the clients during any one year, how many families were reunited, or how much physical or emotional change occurred in which clients.

Measuring agency efficiency requires finding out what staff actually does, the cost per child, and whether the program results can be achieved by reducing the intensity of service or by offering a different type of service such as group homes, short-term placement, or residential centers (Schwartz, 1970).

Agencies need to know not only if they succeed but why. They need to understand which attributes of a program make it more or less successful, and which clients do best under what conditions. In addition to suggesting what facts might be gathered, a subcommittee of a professional association could clarify the issues in foster care for the media and specify what knowledge already exists that might help clarify the issues (Kadushin, 1971).

The professional association might also assist the agencies in developing evaluations. It is extremely difficult to establish indices of change or success. Reuniting a family is not the only valid criteria of success in foster care. Outcome studies can also be extremely complex to carry out (Suchman, 1967). Time, acceptable degree of specificity, and money must all be considered.

Rivlin (1971, pp. 142–143) makes the point that single measures of social service performance should be avoided. Judging a foster care agency solely on the basis of uniting families can lead to administrative distortion or cheating to beat the system. Single measures do not take into account the multiple goals of agencies or what they have to work with.

Multiple measures, weighted in terms of agency priorities, are required. Such performance measures should not only reflect qualitative standards of success (such as the reunification of families at acceptable levels of functioning), but also must take into account the quantity of service the agency is expected to provide. These measures should also reflect something about the difficulty of the task and its cost.

No organization really can achieve 100 percent of its goals. There are both internal and external reasons for this fact. The requisite knowledge is seldom available, the resources needed are generally inadequate, the sanction to act is limited. In addition, an organization must expend some of its resources to recruit additional resources, to provide for the morale of its employees, and to prepare for contingencies (Etzioni, 1960).

If goal attainment is the only standard of evaluation, organizations fail before they start. What must be done is to calculate the optimal level of goal attainment possible given the constraints imposed by the organization's need for survival and its need for the adaptability to meet the exigencies of the unpredictable environment in which it must operate.

Discussion

Instituting a get the facts campaign will not necessarily lead to useful changes. Vigilance concerning the process and procedures of evaluation is required. Administrators are sorely tempted to resort to devious measures, especially when they feel outside groups have hidden agendas or are out to destroy or control their agencies.

Walker (1972, p. 53) noted "by careful avoidance of recidivist-prone clients . . . many programs appear to be scoring high on program benefits. . . . A second alternative . . . is to reduce the volume of clients served. . . . A third method of obtaining spurious benefits involves the point in time when benefit measures are applied . . . measuring outcomes before the client loses them. . . . A final method . . . setting goals that are easy to achieve or defining client status-at-entry as lower than it actually is."

Yet, it is not only administration that must be watched; it is also the staff and the board. Numerous studies have shown that staff in social agencies prefer symbolic research to actual evaluatory research (Eaton, 1962). Because it is difficult to isolate the effect of agency from other factors which influence clients, staff could be unjustly blamed for poor results. Indices of success or change are often unreliable. The consequences of research are not immediately apparent or useful. And, even the youngest and most self-effacing staff member feels he knows that unless jobs are available, there is not much that can be done for clients, so why involve the agency in more fact-gathering.

Even a well-trained, truly representative board will be loathe to make known the results of fact-gathering if the agency's survival is at stake. Can the board really risk the public's understanding of a three-month intensive evaluation when all the public does is glance at a three-inch column in the newspaper or a squib on television? A board is more likely to make public evaluatory statements based on historical improvement of the agency or on comparisons with other agencies. Or, focus statements on areas of concern to funding groups (efficiency of operation, research grants received, and discharge rates) in any particular year (Thompson, 1967, pp. 83–89). Thus, it may be necessary in the short run to have public and private evaluations. In the long run, a climate must be built up both inside and outside the agency that allows truth to surface without the threat of devastating consequences (Rosenblatt, 1968).

It is incumbent on lower level staff to be sophisticated in their approach to agency evaluations. They must know how to minimize risks by urging common appraisals of whole systems. Judgments will have to be made concerning how prudent certain risks are. There can be considerable disagreement between staff and administration on these matters. Yet, there is no way to avoid the necessity of making judgments in organizational life, especially judgments about the timing and extent of disclosure of information.

Some people believe that insufficient sharing of information may be the main problem in organizational life. If only everyone would give everyone else all the information at their disposal, then there would be no difficulties in organizational life.

This is a vast oversimplification. There is often insufficient time to share all the information that is required when a task must be done quickly. Nor does everyone want to know everything that is going on. People depend on others to define most issues for them, with attendant distortion. Information takes on different meanings to different levels of staff, depending on their personal interests and their position in the organization. And, the essence of organizational life is judgment and not fact. With judgment there can be legitimate differences of opinion.

If the judgment of the boss about whether to take a particular course of action is critical, then one wishes the judgment to be favorable to one's own position. Therefore, one stalks the lion, one makes judgments about when and what to disclose. If it is not important how the judgment comes out or how strains among goals are resolved, then one can afford the luxury of the position that one should never influence another person through any means other than rational persuasion.

Admittedly, there are problems with the manipulation of people and information. The pacifist viewpoint is held by many: manipulation (war) cannot bring about a situation where rationality (peace) will prevail. If one believes in just wars in organizations, then manipulation will be used. Nevertheless, wars should be the last recourse. The degree of manipulation is always at issue.

Lower level staff may feel that the tactics suggested to clean up an agency mess will take a long time. Social workers may not want to get involved in such difficult, time-consuming, and intricate procedures. Many workers want to go to a staff meeting, state their point of view, have the staff vote, and have the change instituted— all in one hour and forty-five minutes on Monday morning. These workers would be better advised to settle back into a job that they enjoy and make their peace with the existing organization. Cheap changes are generally only minor ones. Lasting change takes time and commitment. There are good reasons why both people and agencies change slowly.

8

Understanding the Budget

Those who give money to social agencies have influence over them. The precise type and degree of influence is a matter for discovery, as is the manner in which the agency gets its money. For example, if each department chief recruits his own funds from different sources, the executive director has considerably less power over the departmental chiefs than if all the funds came from a central source.

A Do-Good Organizational Secret: Money is not given simply to do good, money is given to do what somebody thinks is good.

The necessity of getting the money to run an agency is the strongest pressure on administrators. Workers seldom feel this pressure. Therefore, under normal circumstances they give little consideration to the way their agencies are funded.

Scope of the Problem

When Louise Benjamin walked into Maimonides Hospital on her first day of field work, money was the farthest thing from her mind. Louise had never been away from home for any length of time, and life in a strange big city was quite an adjustment. The hospital seemed exciting.

Maimonides is located on the edge of the civic center area and on the boundary of the black ghetto of a midwestern city. The hospital had been started in the late nineteenth century by Jewish philanthropists to serve the then growing Jewish community. Throughout the years it has maintained a reputation for excellence in medicine as well as in research. There has always been a close working relationship and interchange of staff with the medical school of a nearby university.

Although the board of directors at Maimonides is still composed of representatives of the older Jewish families who founded the hospital, they no longer provide the bulk of the funds. Some funds come from the Federation of Jewish Philanthropies which makes a joint fund-raising appeal for all of its member agencies once a year. A small part of funds comes from private endowments. The bulk of funds comes from patient fees in the form of reimbursements from Blue Cross and Blue Shield.

For her first two weeks, Louise was given an orientation to the hospital. It was just like in the movies, bright corridors, the chime of the bells, and calls for doctors wanted in mysterious services. Louise learned a great deal about the complex hospital policies and procedures at training institutes. The board of directors sets these policies and procedures. The board also hires the hospital administrator who runs the hospital. The administrator is Stephen Goldfarb, a man in his early fifties who started out in medicine to be a pediatrician, but got involved in hospital administration. He has not seen patients for well over twenty years. His suite on the ground floor also houses the director of maintenance, the comptroller, the personnel director, the director of research, and all of their staffs.

Goldfarb's assistant, Levin, has a master's degree in hospital administration and actually runs the hospital. Goldfarb spends his time raising money.

The hospital is divided into various services. The chiefs of these services meet every other week with the hospital administrator and make decisions concerning the utilization of hospital facilities. They are also consulted by the administrator in developing the yearly budget.

Yet money affects relationships between departments and professions. This is certainly the case in hospitals. With a fixed budget, if more social workers are hired there is less money available for doctors and nurses.

In this chapter the role relationships between doctors and social workers are analyzed. While factors other than money are important in determining these relationships, ultimately changes in roles and functions must be translated into dollars and cents. Budgets reflect not only what jobs there are but also the importance accorded to these jobs.

The wards have a hierarchy of their own. There are medical students, interns, residents, attending doctors, the patients' private doctors, and the chief of service whose job it is to oversee this whole arrangement. There are also nurses, head nurses, nurses' aides, and attendants.

Two years ago, the chief of social service was invited to sit on the utilization committee. Prior to this, only the chiefs of the medical services, all doctors, served on the committee. Now the chief of nursing service and the chief of physical therapy also serve.

The social service department is headed by Ms. Berglinder. Highly respected, Ms. Berglinder has written several articles and a text on medical casework.

Over the years, the social service department had grown considerably. There are now twenty-two M.S.W.s working in various services at Maimonides. Ms. Berglinder is not actually the superior of all the workers. For example, the social workers assigned to pediatrics take their orders from the doctors. Yet, Ms. Berglinder passes on their promotions and salary increases and writes their letters of recommendation.

The local school of social work has always been one of the major training centers for medical caseworkers in the country. Louise learned a great deal about the psychosomatic aspects of illness, the reactions of clients in hospitals to disabling and chronic illnesses, and how the caseworker can help a patient to understand his emotional reactions and to return to some degree of normal functioning. She was particularly interested in the effect of hospitalization on children. Every other week a well-known doctor lectured on some medical problem and its attendant emotional manifestations. Yet, the course in medical casework was not completely relevant to Louise's work at Maimonides.

Louise's first case involved post-op service. Her patient had had his right leg amputated. The patient was quite depressed and would need a great deal of assistance before discharge and his convalescing at home. Louise was told to make provisions for him to be taken care of in the community. He was to be discharged in two days and he had no family. Louise took the case to the head social worker and was told that many patients are lethargic and depressed after an operation. Louise learned in subsequent months that the surgical unit is only interested in training young surgeons. Therefore, they need the bed space. Amputees are not kept in the hospital any longer than absolutely necessary for medical treatment. She found the same problem in several of the other services. They only cared about interesting cases for teaching. If you are not an interesting case, you are in bad shape.

The hospital put a high premium on research, because of its affiliation with the university and its self-appointed mission of adding to medical knowledge. Also, every research grant included money (up to 35 percent of the grant) for indirect costs which went to the hospital to pay for overhead—rental of facilities, electricity, telephone, part of the financial and personnel department salaries, and part of the hospital administrator's salary.

An older caseworker told Louise that the hospital's agenda was research first, doctors' training second, maintenance of the hospital third, and patient care last. All she had to do was compare wards where research was going on and similar wards where there was no research. Research wards had more facilities, equipment, and staff.

The doctors involved in the intensive care unit had very little idea of what social work was all about. The head social worker on the unit played handmaiden to the doctors. Social workers were there to do whatever the doctors wanted.

One of the most dissatisfied workers said, "We are the bottom of the ladder. The doctors see us as getting people out, as clerks. Social workers do everything but sweep the floor. Our job is to keep the doctor happy." Just the week before Louise had heard a lecture on the medical team and how it functioned. She wondered if the lecturer had ever actually worked in a hospital.

The way money is secured to pay social workers creates part of the problem. Maimonides is reimbursed by Blue Cross for its patient care. Blue Cross rates its hospitals in terms of standards of good service, one standard being the ratio of social workers to patients. If Maimonides has a social worker for X number of patients, it receives X number of dollars more per patient than it would if it did not have a social worker. Doctors do not necessarily want social workers, but the hospital administration does.

The importance of money was evident elsewhere. Every department and every service in the hospital was fighting every other service over allocations of beds, space, clerical assistants, and supplies. Every service wants more space and the hospital simply has a finite amount of it.

Two nurses Louise became friendly with, Ms. Haley and Ms. Mason, explained the situation to her. There is a whole status system in the hospital involving the various services. The services are aware of the need for cooperation, but money problems change everything. Whenever there is a financial squeeze, social services are vulnerable. They are not strong enough to make the hospital administrator maintain their budget allocation. The heads of the medical services have board contacts and can create great difficulty for the administrator; and, the prestigious doctors are not bothered by budget cuts. The fighting between departments has a long history at Maimonides and has a great effect on what can and cannot be done. There are many grudges and scores waiting to be settled.

Resistance to Change

The best way to understand the hospital is to see the various services as political parties. Money is the precious metal of social agencies, and organizational politics is the refining process. Ms. Berglinder played politics and won a place on the utilization and patient care committee.

The previous chief of social service used denial and seduction to deal with the problems on the wards. She simply told workers that doctors must make the decisions on the ward. If the worker would establish a good relationship with the doctor, everything could be worked out. This infuriated the workers. They were left no avenues for expressing their ideas and opinions.

Ms. Berglinder first moved to establish the competence of the social service department. She knew that social service had something to offer in the hospital and set about proving this to those doctors who had power on the patient care and utilization committee. To be able to trade and bargain one must have something to trade.

While she proved to them that social work could produce, she also got the message across that she was a person who could be trusted. The more useful social service became, the more powerful it actually became. Social service became more in evidence as Ms. Berglinder was allowed to hire an increasing number of social workers.

Ms. Berglinder was not timid. The chief of the TB ward had been particularly abusive to one of the social workers. When discussions failed, Ms. Berglinder simply pulled the workers off the ward. This created quite a row but the word was soon out. Ms. Berglinder had already developed her alliances, including a talk with the director of personnel. Ms. Berglinder was good at bargaining, and there were innumerable opportunities.

> *Each department exercises a near monopoly over a specialized resource or skill (x-ray, pathology, surgery), without which the hospital cannot function. . . . The hospital is a network of interlocking power centers or empires, each of which is struggling to preserve its autonomy and maintain its own boundaries while at the same time it is attempting to increase its own share of institutional resources, space, money, and the like, as well as its influence in policy making. . . . The chief(s) can add to this power by entering into coalitions or ad hoc alliances with other department heads, trading power, contracting and discharging obligations, thus producing a flexible, subtle but potent informal power structure. . . . The most important reason for the increasing stature of social work in the hospital is the*

enormous change in the organization and distribution of medical services. . . . As medical care becomes more closely woven into the social fabric of society, social work becomes an integral rather than an additive function in the medical organization [Wax, 1968, p. 66].

Ms. Berglinder deployed the social workers in such a manner as to increase her power. Pediatric services were interested in utilizing social workers for the maximal benefits of the patients through mutually discussing what social work could and could not do. They were rewarded with more workers and more attention. Yet, there are problems related to hospital politics. Much of political maneuvering must be hidden, and Ms. Berglinder could not share it with her staff.

One staff member said that Ms. Berglinder spent more time politicking and intriguing than developing the social work skills and techniques of the staff. The staff complained that they never really knew what was happening in the hospital. Many were upset when they heard things through the rumor mill rather than from Ms. Berglinder. A few of the supervisors understood exactly what Ms. Berglinder was doing. Ms. Abramson, Louise's training supervisor, practiced the same art.

Amy Abramson got along well on the wards because of her vivacious personality and because she acted as the informal social worker to the staff. Anybody who had a problem in his family or on the job knew that he could talk to Amy. These incurred obligations paid off handsomely for her when she needed things done. She used informal contacts with staff to help in the training of the social work students. However, this ward healer technique leaves untouched the total organizational situation which causes the problems. It is unlikely that all workers can practice Amy Abramson's art, simply because they may not have the institutional access to resources or the personality to play the role.

Strategy

Most social service departments operate on the style set in 1905 when the first medical social workers were hired at Massachusetts General Hospital in Boston. Social workers operate in services at the behest of physicians. They take referrals from the doctors and do not do their own case-finding. This is a completely different system than when the social worker talks to the patients on the ward and suggests possible services to the doctor that the worker might perform to aid the patient. Most medical caseworkers feel that the latter style is the more appropriate one.

Most doctors have only the vaguest notion of what social workers can do because they have had little contact with social workers. To teach doctors how to use social workers, workers must show the doctor what they can do rather than ask the doctor what to do. This depends on the worker's ability to develop a reputation for competence. The doctor has to make the final decisions about medical care, but social workers must provide information to help him make the best decisions.

Amy Abramson realized that doctors develop their ideas about social work from what they see social workers do. "If they think we are clerks, it is because most of our contact with them is around filling out papers."

Formally, she began structuring situations so that doctors had to sit in on discussions with the families of patients. Informally, she placed herself near the coffee machine after rounds. More and more she became party to the discussions about patients which occurred over coffee. Amy had set up an educational process which began with interaction and ended many months later in a series of formal training sessions and discussions of doctor–social worker cooperation.

Amy's first years as a social worker had been filled with arguing and complaining. Then she began to fit her tactics to the doctors. Arguing on the basis of good patient care antagonized doctors who were supposedly the best judge of this.

Amy discovered that most doctors are anxious to have a smooth functioning ward. Therefore, rather than argue that a particular patient should not be moved out, she insisted that sufficient notice was necessary for the social workers to make appropriate contacts in the community. Rushing after the doctors to find time to discuss things with them was inefficient and wasteful. She pointed this out over and over again and ultimately secured a regular meeting time.

Amy developed one basic rule in working with the doctors: never let a doctor dictate the solution to a social service problem.

If a doctor came to Amy and told her to place a patient in a nursing home, she asked whether he had considered several other possible solutions.

Doctors often know little about community resources. Nor do they appreciate the importance of involving the patient in planning for his recuperation. Amy always acknowledged the importance of moving patients out of the hospital and then explained what was involved in this process, especially the importance of making plans with the patient. Gradually, doctors began to understand what social workers do and do not do.

Amy was also instrumental in getting the hospital to hire an ombudsman. Any patient who had a complaint could ask to see the ombudsman. Amy suggested that the ombudsman actually query each patient, not necessarily personally, but through forms, for suggestions and experiences in the hospital. By doing this, she insured that the ombudsman would receive compliments as well as complaints about the hospital. A mechanism was created for feedback of this information to the various departments.

The ombudsman system depends on the capacity and will of the hospital administrator to utilize the information. If the information were sent to the board, it might be put to better use.

Nevertheless, the institution of the ombudsman has had a liberating effect on the line staff. The major problem, staffs say, is that most chiefs of service demand what they call "loyalty" from their staff. If the chiefs of service emphasize the teaching aspects of the hospital, they do not wish their staff to undermine or argue with their priority. Often on a service there are conflicts between doctors. The doctor whose ward a social worker is on will not tolerate the worker informing the chief of service that he is holding beds for particular types of patients even though the chief of service had indicated clearly that he was opposed to this practice. The liberating effect occurs when workers see practices that are contrary to stated policy and simply mention to patients that they can talk with the ombudsman. This lever considerably pyramids the workers' power.

Discussion

Decisions about what is best medically for a patient must be made by doctors. Decisions about who gets into the hospital and who gets preferential treatment are not medical decisions, but decisions which must be made by the community and its representatives. As the organization and delivery of health services change in our society, medical training will change to fit the new circumstances. Social workers will play an increasingly important part in health services. The days of social worker as handmaiden are clearly numbered. The bases on which departmental politics are played in a hospital have shifted.

Yet, there is danger that in any shift to community health, social workers will use their increased influence to improve the quality of social services rather than to improve the quality of hospital services. Considering the health of the whole community a hospital serves, an expanded outpatient department might be more important than improving the quality of social services. A truly representative board of directors must make such decisions; otherwise, it will be business as usual with social workers in a slightly better position in the money and power battles.

An agency's budget is its ego. It acts differently, depending on whether it gets its funds from private donations, the public treasury, fees for service, or time-delimited grants. No one can be successful in changing an organization without becoming proficient in budget psychology (Argyris, 1970).

Some lower level staff despair of ever changing the way agencies like hospitals function. They advocate a system of providing clients with the money to pay for services. In hospitals this would mean that every patient would be able to pay for the absolute best in medical care. Client choice would eliminate ineffective agencies (Reid, 1972).

There is no way social institutions can avoid being constrained by their need for money and survival. The question is one of degree and essential purpose (Beck, 1969).

9

Participating in Management

This concluding case study discusses the issue of staff participation in the management of social agencies. While each of the prior cases in some fashion has dealt with this issue, this chapter looks at the general problems such participation can present. Should there be limits on staff participation? Are power struggles the inevitable result of such participation? Can leadership function without discretionary power?

A community mental health center serves as the context for discussion. The intent of the federal act which authorizes community mental health centers is the provision of comprehensive psychiatric services under one central authority for jurisdictions of one hundred thousand or larger. A mental health center must by law have a board composed of citizens and professionals. Initially, the board must draw up plans for the center and submit a proposal for funding. Once plans are approved by the National Institute of Mental Health, the board is responsible for policy-setting and overseeing a center's operation. Since an inpatient service is required, each mental health center must be affiliated with a hospital.

Scope of the Problem

Gonzaga State Community Mental Health Center is located in a far western city. Gonzaga State is headed by Whitman Tower, an ambitious man who has extensive contacts at the state capitol. Tower is a national officer of the American Psychiatric Association and hopes to become state commissioner of mental health. He is not a man to miss the significance of bills passed in the state legislature or Congress pertaining to mental health.

The Community Mental Health Act meant money and the opportunity to expand his program from a three-hundred-bed inpatient hospital and small outpatient service to a comprehensive program that included day care facilities, child guidance clinics, and an extensive community education program. Tower liked to look at the buildings at Gonzaga and feel that they were his. He found the private practice of psychiatry boring. The emotional reward of helping a patient was nothing compared to the feelings he got when he walked around the wards of the hospital and all the personnel and patients acknowledged his presence.

He quickly set about organizing a mental health center board. It included several of the members of his hospital board plus some other leading citizens who had a known interest in mental health. With his usual efficiency, the proposal was written in three months and was one of the first funded in the country.

The program was to be experimental, with two satellite clinics located in the slum areas of the city. These clinics would operate on a twenty-four hour basis, take care of emergencies, and offer traditional and nontraditional types of therapy. Local citizens who showed an empathy and a desire to work with others would be given on-the-job training to do group counseling.

The proposal called for a five-year program. For the first two years the budget provided a capital fund of over a million dollars plus an operating budget of three hundred seventy-five thousand dollars for each year. The funds would be administered by the mental health board. Tower would serve as executive director of the center as well as continue as director of the hospital. It was understood that after two years the positions would be split.

Once the proposal was funded, expansion at Gonzaga was quick and impressive. William Wetson, a young psychiatrist who had worked with the poverty program in San Francisco, was hired as the director of community psychiatry. His staff was to include, for each of the two proposed satellite clinics, a staff psychiatrist, five social workers, a psychologist, two nurses, and ten case aides.

The director of the west side satellite clinic was William Caroll. He was a traditional psychiatrist—he saw therapy basically as occurring in a one-to-one relationship or a group relationship—and he organized the center in traditional ways. The psychologist did testing, the nurses gave medication, the social workers dealt with families, the psychiatrist gave therapy and prescribed medication to the more severe cases, and the case aides assisted the social workers.

The director of the east side clinic, John McDonald, believed there were a great many ways to help people. Feeling that it was unrealistic to assume that sufficient psychiatrists could be trained to do the job, he encouraged his entire staff to participate in developing the administrative structure of the clinic. All service and clerical staff attended small group meetings and had an equal vote. Every service staff member, regardless of discipline or level of training, was to be a primary therapist for a certain number of patients. Therapists would have ultimate clinical responsibility for the patients. Thus, everyone—whether clinician, administrator, or student—would directly experience the problems in dealing with clients.

The east side staff manual stated: "Any employee can initiate proposals to establish new policies or change existing policies. To avoid lengthy discussions and impulsive proposals, proposals must be in writing and placed on the agenda for staff meetings in advance. All topics placed on the agenda must be discussed. If staff approves a proposal it can be vetoed by the center director, provided he waits ten days and presents a written statement to the staff on his reason for the veto."

Terry Simon had been a social worker in the outpatient clinic at Gonzaga State for six years. Although an excellent therapist, he was difficult to get along with. He had had innumerable fights with the administration, but remained at the hospital because he enjoyed his work with schizophrenics. He had a special knack for communicating with the most uncommunicative patients.

Terry was particularly outspoken about the administration of the hospital whom he referred to as "psycosa nostra." When Tower took over the hospital, he brought an assistant director with him. They began their administration in an extremely aggressive, calculated manner. In this way, they were able to ascertain which of the department heads could be counted as loyal to Tower and his new administration, and which could not.

Tower demanded that the chief of social service transfer five workers from one unit of the hospital to another. Adequate time was not allowed for discussion and negotiation. If the chief of social service had not acquiesced, she would have been threatened with dismissal. In other cases, transfer to undesirable units in the hospital was threatened. If a department chief did not respond in the manner desired, he found himself uninvited to department meetings. After six months, Tower had a mafia, a group of people who were loyal to him and not to the clients or the organization, and who were rewarded for this loyalty. Those who did not accede were either forced to leave or simply ignored in the operation of the hospital. The chief of social service played the game.

She was a middle-aged woman who was frightened to death of Tower. Nevertheless, she seemed to take to the mafia way of administration. Private deals were made with staff. Certain people had the right to work four days a week, others had access to clients to set up private practices. Terry would have none of this. When Terry heard about John McDonald and the east side clinic, he quickly applied for a transfer.

Resistance to Change

John McDonald was a decent person. Terry both respected him and saw him as a lamb being led to the slaughter. McDonald instinctively realized that Terry was a man to be trusted, but believed him to be much too cynical. Nevertheless, McDonald was anxious that Terry become a member of the staff.

McDonald spent a great deal of time thinking about various innovative treatment modalities. He was particularly intrigued by an idea called Theory Y or management by objectives (McGregor, 1960).

The main tenets of the theory are: increased decentralization of power and delegation of responsibility, enlargement of the scope of most jobs, employee participation and consultative management, and performance appraisals in which the employee does most of the appraising. The theory assumes that professionalization, specialization, and the need for innovation are at odds with traditional bureaucratic functioning. Rules and regulations only work well when an organization is carrying out routine and repetitive tasks.

To Terry, the theory was everything he had always been arguing for. However, he really did not believe it could work. He decided to do some library research on experiments with Theory Y, and he sent the following memo to McDonald (adapted from Wilcox, 1969): "My research has led me to conclude that Theory Y has important possibilities for the functioning of our center. I think it can increase initiative, foster self-reliance, and lead to more effective and efficient service if we keep several vital cautions in mind.

"Some writers seem to think that increased participation, better means of communicating among workers, more self-control, and reduced authority in an organization are desirable as ends in themselves, regardless of their organizational consequences, that is, effectiveness. This is a luxury our clients cannot afford. It also represents just the situation we are trying to correct, an agency that works well for the staff but not for the clients. The implication is that everyone must like or approve of what they are doing. This is impossible. What happens to the clients rather than a worker's ability to self-actualize himself is the crucial variable. Resolution of the strain between efficiency and self-actualization is a matter of degree. We should err on the side of what happens to clients. Endless discussions with workers is destructive of morale. Some authority will be required.

"The crucial issue is not so much reduced authority as it is increased accountability. Democratic decision-making is considerably easier than democratic monitoring of the implementation of decisions. Peers have great difficulty regulating peers. Once objectives are set, the organization must have an institutionalized way of seeing that the objectives are met.

"There is a tendency in some of the reports to downgrade the need for expertise. They seem to imply that expertise is easy to develop and that group decision-making can be a good substitute. Serious professionals who indeed are experts are not going to sit back and let a group make decisions simply because it is good for a group to learn from its mistakes. More likely, they will play politics. There is a strain between expertise and participative management.

"In real life there often is not enough time to share all information and go through the laborious process of informing everyone. Some actions must be taken quickly, like getting in a grant proposal. There is then a tendency or real necessity to bring the staff along.

"Not everyone really wants to participate; yet, everyone has a whole series of demands—personal and professional—not all of which can be considered. Aggression and hostility are the result. One of the functions of the traditional bureaucratic hierarchy is to absorb hostility. Institutionalized methods of handling hostility must be created that do not immobilize an organization. Direct democracy can lead to factionalism and immobilization."

McDonald was impressed by the memo, particularly the discussion of politics. He had kept for himself the power of veto. Without this power he would have become a discussion leader rather than a leader. Terry's advice was: set up a system whereby consensus can develop around the best informed judgments concerning the facts of particular situations, but maintain the power to decide if and when consensus cannot be developed.

Given the state of knowledge in the mental health field, there is no way of doing away with the need for making informed judgments. Institutionalizing voting as a means of decision-making, rather than viewing voting as an act of seeing if there is consensus, leads to the formation of political parties and party lines. "You support my judgment on this issue and I'll support yours on that issue." Thus, decisions tend to be made on political grounds, and actual results are overlooked if unfavorable to long-range ends. It is not what you say but who you are sitting with that becomes important.

The institutionalization of politics in a setting where knowledge and competence must reign is the antithesis of such rational ends. Propaganda and stereotyping become the rule. There will always be a degree of politicking. The issue is to keep it within bounds. To achieve this, the assessment of results must be institutionalized.

Even with all of Terry's warnings, McDonald wrote the following in a confidential summary of the first nine months' operation to Weston (Enelow and Weston, 1971):

"In keeping with our philosophy that nurses are trained to do more than they are ordinarily permitted to do, we assigned several key administrative functions to them. Ordinarily, these are functions performed by psychiatrists. After a few months, some puzzling inconsistencies began to appear in our records, particularly in regard to after-care and consultation. Investigation turned up the fact that several ambitious and energetic young psychiatric nurses, in concert with their peers at other institutions around the community, had developed a parallel community mental health center organization made up exclusively of nurses. This shadow community mental health center was functioning in our center but basically independent of it."

The issue was not so much what the nurses did, but that there was no way of holding them accountable. What if what they were doing was not working? How could the other services of the center gain their cooperation? This clearly was not what expanding the scope of job responsibilities was meant to achieve. Some unanticipated variables had intervened.

Terry also pointed out that Theory Y was developed by businessmen. It is based on an incentive plan that allocates bonuses to work groups in terms of their increased productivity or time- or money-saving innovations. This plan would be difficult to translate to service organizations. Giving merit increases only to exceptional staff disrupts a team or work group. The alternative of paying people initially an adequate salary was impossible because McDonald could only recommend that a social worker be hired at a particular salary level. The chief of social service retained the power of hiring and granting salary increases.

The situation with the clerical and case aide staff was more crucial. They were being asked to do a great deal. The only way to get around their low salaries was to hire them originally at the higher steps of their job category. How long would these workers sustain their involvement when McDonald was unable to give them anything but verbal rewards?

At his regular Monday meeting with Wetson, McDonald complained that the administrative arrangement over promotions was not conducive to the operation of the satellite center as he envisioned it. Wetson was a more sophisticated administrator than McDonald, having lived through the poverty programs. He decided to support McDonald mainly because he felt he needed as much authority and control as possible to really make the clinics operate. Thus, when he presented his case to Tower, he stated that both Caroll and McDonald refused to operate under such a decision.

The mafia understands that it has to pay a price for carrying out its activities. It must give just enough so that a revolt is not engendered, but not enough to lose what it wants.

Tower allowed salary increases for social workers and psychologists, but held the line on the clericals, citing civil service. He did not wish to relinquish this source of control. Since little effort is put into assessing the results achieved by an agency, a therapeutic mafia can base its decisions on maintaining control and furthering whatever ends it thinks enhances this control. There is no one to hold them to account.

Terry also mentioned the problem of maintenance of the facility, a problem McDonald had never given a second thought to. He was concerned about clinical therapeutic effects. Satellite clinics were cleaned and maintained through the central maintenance service of Gonzaga State. McDonald responded to maintenance problems by sending a memo, and then another memo, then phone calls to Wetson, and finally a call to Tower which, of course, was not answered.

Maintenance departments are generally understaffed and constantly subject to the demands of others. Maintenance men, just as social workers, desire to control their jobs. They develop techniques for toning down the constant sense of emergency which emanates from every department every time they are called. Maintenance has no way of evaluating whether it is more important to place a light bulb in the east side clinic or replace a lock on the closed ward. McDonald failed to realize that when a director cannot get the toilet fixed, the staff begins to think of him in toilet terms.

Strategy

The problems with maintenance men, lack of supplies, and inadequate secretarial service can seldom be dealt with on a departmental basis. McDonald, Caroll, and Wetson together might have made some impact.

When dealt with by a single department, these things get better temporarily, then revert to their same old status. The conditions which cause the problem—whether they be inadequate personnel, poor policy and procedures, or insufficient resources—have not been altered. The system can accommodate or temporarily handle problems in one of its departments, and it does. But, when the situation reverts to its prior poor state, someone else is being accommodated.

Central administration seldom feels the pinch of poor maintenance and poor resources. They get the best. The director of maintenance knows that when the boss calls he must get there immediately. Thus, if rationality and concerted effort fail, pressure must be brought to bear. The boss must be made to feel the pinch.

Liberation is a game developed in the army. It should not be played by everyone. For some, it may be as distasteful as war itself. Nonetheless, it can accomplish certain objectives. Its basic rule is this: If someone steals something from you, you steal something from him. In an agency there is a slight variation. If you need something and cannot get it, you take it from the boss' office.

Liberation is not an end in itself. Its purpose is to make the central office feel the problems that you feel. Admittedly, liberation is a little hard to carry out with electric typewriters. Yet, commando raids can make negotiations over policy and procedure take on a new tone.

There are, of course, the timid who are afraid to play liberation. They play other games, such as hoarding, blackmarketing, and bribing. For them, there is nothing like slipping the maintenance men a bottle of whiskey.

There is a tendency in social agencies to look upon people who engage in organizational maneuvering, of which the above is a simple example, as power mad or power hungry. Certainly, there are people like this; yet, power struggles occur too frequently for this diagnosis to be accurate.

The real pleasure of power is the pleasure of freedom, and it goes back to one of man's most primitive needs, the need to control his environment. What you want is the freedom to carry out your ideas. The problem, of course, is that everybody else wants the same. There are hundreds of little power struggles going on in an organization. To a certain extent, they are all played according to the same rules. Those at the top offer the most dramatic illustration (Jay, 1969, pp. 40–47).

Soon after his arrival at Gonzaga, Wetson entered into a power struggle with Tower. First, he overspent his budget. If one can get away with it, then one begins to take other advantages. Wetson got away with it simply because Tower was afraid to jeopardize the grant. He made money available from unspent funds from another source.

Wetson was encouraged to be bolder. He began to withhold information and to delay coordinating the work of the satellite centers with the hospital. Tower quickly formed an alliance with Caroll, the director of the west side satellite center, whose traditional style made him a natural ally. With a direct pipeline to one of Wetson's underlings, Tower considerably curtailed Wetson's maneuverability.

Tower had available a number of tactics which he did not have to use. In prior years he had dealt with a recalcitrant department chief by temporarily assigning one of his henchmen to run the department on the ruse of a research project he invented. When things got tough, Tower trotted out his rubber stamp board of directors as a show of power. He ultimately used the budget to knock a few more bricks out of a usurper's castle, i.e., cutting a few budget lines, building of competing departments, and the like.

The reason Wetson entered into the power struggle was that he had a diametrically opposed view of administration than Tower. Tower believed in hierarchy, strict procedures, and accountability. Wetson wanted to set up a cellular system of organization in the mental health center.

A hierarchical organization is based on discrete units. There, a hospital is organized into various services—inpatient, day residence, emergency and outpatient service. Each department or division is responsible for particular processes. The army is the prototype of such a structure.

The cellular structure, rather than being concerned with a particular process, is concerned with a product. Each cellular structure would entail several wards who received their patients from a particular area in the city. There would be a team related to health education in that area. There would be staff involved in utilizing the community as a treatment resource. There would be an emergency service related to that area, and there would be a residence related to that area. Everyone in the cell is related to what occurs to the patients rather than solely to discrete pieces of the process such as group counseling. Size is the crucial variable. Smallness is important so that the interchange of ideas and experience can occur.

Wetson's plan would considerably reduce the number of supervisors and middle management personnel. It would flatten out the pyramid. The cells would be given a budget and a set of objectives. The head office would hold the cells accountable for meeting these objectives. Total planning for all the cells or the total community mental health center would be carried out by a program advisory council made up of representatives from the cells.

At Gonzaga Terry knew that he had to take a position in relation to this power struggle. The disagreements were too profound to be bridged. Yet, staff would be well advised to be wary of hasty involvement. Wisdom and virtue are often not on the same side. Wetson, as will be noted, was a poor contender.

Power struggles are the inevitable result of parties who seek freedom of action. Since there is considerable room for honest as well as selfish disagreement in social agencies, they are to be expected. While it is impossible to give precise rules as to how these struggles should be fought or what lower level staff should do, from remaining neutral to playing each side off against the other, one caveat is in order.

While it is unlikely in the short run in the heat of controversy to tell if clients benefit, in the long run a means of making this judgment must be devised. Irresponsibility lies not in being on the wrong side but remaining on it. Since lower level staff are seldom the main contenders in power struggles, they may be well situated to insist on a focus on clients.

Discussion

An inaccessible and entrenched administration is a formidable barrier to a line worker. It is highly unlikely that this administration can be changed from within. Certainly, Wetson wasn't able to do it and he operated from a position of considerable power.

McDonald provided Wetson with a potentially powerful tool for dislodging the administration when he began to form a community board for the east side clinic. The board was formed to advise the clinic on its operation. It was comprised of residents of the east side, people who could not afford a private psychiatrist and were potential consumers of the services of the center.

Wetson did not understand how to develop such a citizen's group. He found, for example, that because people came to one meeting, they did not necessarily come back. He also found that members of the group did not have sufficient knowledge and information about mental health to make judgments on their own. Nevertheless, Wetson decided to use this group in an attempt to force the overall board to consider his ideas.

A confrontation occurred at a joint meeting with the overall community board. The board agreed to study Wetson's ideas. Delay occurred, some of the local citizens stopped coming to the east side clinic monthly meetings, and two months after the confrontation Tower organized his own consumer advisory board. Wetson resigned shortly after this.

Wetson's training had simply not equipped him with the techniques and processes necessary for a knockdown organizational fight. He saw meetings as confrontations where ideas are thought out, issues clarified, and solutions developed. That meetings and confrontations are often only symbolic expressions of a whole series of actions which have gone on and been staged to lead up to the meeting never occurred to him. He had never thought about the tactics and strategy of building alliances, neutralizing the opposition, appealing to cherished values, escalating demands, anticipating retaliation, and maintaining support (Alinsky, 1971). He could have benefited from Bill Johnson's orchestration in public welfare of Concerned MSWs, the union, the media, the professional association, and client groups.

All Wetson wanted was a board who would foster his policies. In some ways he was no different than Tower. He just wanted the freedom to do what he thought was best.

What is a well-meaning executive like Wetson to do? Dealing with uncertainty is the essence of administration. To deal with uncertainty, executives must be able to take risks without immediate threat of reprisal, get the resources they require, and maintain the stability of the organization. They require discretion in the form of money, commitment, trust, and time.

A Do-Good Organizational Secret: Discretion is the only part of valor those who prepare budgets are concerned about.

The mafia buys discretion at the expense of the clients. Yet, any administrator needs it. Lower level staff must be careful in their efforts to participate in the running of an agency, that they not so severely limit their leaders' discretion that immobilization results. Because some staff do not like an idea does not mean that it should not be tried. It is difficult to put a precise limit on the amount of discretion an administrator requires. That amount which can arbitrarily keep the facts of any situation from being discussed in the organization is too much. When this limit is broached, leadership stops and dictatorship begins.

Many reforming innovators, once empowered, have turned out to be more committed to their innovation than to making known the actual state of its operation. They are all for the assessment of others' ideas, but are not willing to have their own judged.

Many such innovations can be humanistic. Participative management and consumer control are not religious tenets. They are merely innovations to be tried, altered, or discarded if found wanting. Particular care must be taken to consider the values of those involved in power struggles. Beliefs which refuse to yield to outcomes are the cornerstones of authoritarianism.

The Accountable Agency and the Professional Employee

The analysis of goal strains, value conflicts, and other organizational problems have been keyed to discussion of strategies and tactics for overcoming resistance to change. Without the ability to buttress their logical arguments with sources of influences other than rational persuasion, staff workers indeed will be consigned to the role of supplicants. Yet, strategies and tactics are not enough, for wars can be won and the peace lost.

    The aims of the struggle must be clear in advance. Increased influence of lower level staff is of little intrinsic value as such staff are as prone to error as administrative staff. Attaining such short-range goals as getting rid of incompetents, lightening caseloads, and rationalizing procedures has value. Taken alone, however, they are limited objectives and represent a static view of organizational life—that problems can be abstracted and permanently solved.

On the other hand, the systems view, that all problems are interconnected, often seems too global and diffuse for workers to use in dealing with their difficulties. And rightly so, for there is no adequate operational theory of system and subsystem management that can provide definitive answers to specific organizational problems (Georgopoulos, 1970). Yet, concern about systems is necessary as problems indeed are interconnected.

Two systemic aspects of agency functioning have been suggested in the text as the long-range targets of staff concern because of their centrality to organizational functioning—accountability and leadership. Almost every short-range problem that concerns workers will be affected by them.

Accountability

Accountability involves the structuring of roles in the organization (who is accountable to whom, for what); the methods or procedures by which this accountability is determined; and the consequences, desired and undesired, that buttress the accountability. Unless workers attend to this system, problems seemingly solved often revert to their prior state because the conditions which nurtured the problem in the first place are not adequately monitored. As noted, administration is most responsive to staff concerns and agency problems when it itself is held accountable. Workers must concern themselves with the composition of boards of directors and how they function, the performance standards by which the agency is judged, and the consequences for meeting or not meeting such standards. Barbara Hunter's work with boards in her school district offers a number of examples of how staff can affect these procedures.

A commitment to accountability for results is crucial. It

creates a context where a worker can make suggestions, where his suggestions must either stand or fall on their merits. It puts constraints on agencies retreating to either faddism or authority. It tempers professional grandiosity with reality, helps to define competence, and ultimately assists the public in making some appraisal of what do-good organizations can and cannot accomplish.

It can be argued that a focus on accountability will create as many problems as it is intended to solve. Performance standards can become ends in themselves where fulfilling a quota becomes more important than the manner in which it is fulfilled. Disagreements over priorities among goals can create factions among staff and board which can lead to the alteration of facts to suit one's programmatic preferences.

Such situations do not have to occur. A board and staff can develop sophistication about facts and goal attainment. Certainly, the focus on results is not a panacea. Rather, it is a guard rail that throws the agency back on the track when it begins to lose its course. The mere statement of facts does not automatically bring about change. It introduces a dynamic, a constraint against which various forces must play.

Yet, accountability has potential for misuse. Measuring the achievement of objectives can become a tool for control and punishment in the hands of a rigid and incompetent administration. Such administrators may dislike setting objectives but often look forward to providing consequences. Walker (1972, p. 50) points out that "regardless of rewards (or punishments) for . . . performance, an answer must ultimately be provided to the question: 'Just how do I get better results?'." Without such assistance, accountability will be destroyed. Some feedback of information to staff is required if the agency is to utilize its accountability mechanism to improve its effectiveness rather than simply as a source of control.

While staff require a good deal of sophistication about how to set up effective feedback mechanisms (Downs, 1967, pp. 175–190), the essential issue is similar to that with any other innovation, how to induce the administration to institute it.

Workers may often require more influence than they can muster internally to get their agencies to experiment with new feedback or accountability structures and processes. Walker (1972, p.

53) noted that "while some will still maintain that it is love that makes the world go round, more recent thinking suggests that it is really consequences." Considerable external pressure will be required to make agencies feel the consequences of lack of accomplishment. One tool for exerting such pressure deserves reemphasis, as the activation of this tool should be a long-range aim of staff.

Professional associations generally focus on the individual professional worker. The professional association assures the public that its members possess certain skills and adhere to a specific code of ethics. Yet, for many professions the model of practice is not the individual practitioner. The agency or institution is the locus of practice and is a major intervening variable between the worker and his ability to effectively help clients. A professional association should also be concerned with credentialling agencies if it is concerned about what happens to clients. It must indicate to workers that an agency is truly professional.

The National Association of Social Workers now has a code of ethics for individual practitioners to which agencies often subscribe. This code assures clients how they will be treated by their workers. It does not include a set of operating procedures for agencies. Certainly such procedures should include: systematic yearly evaluation of agency effectiveness, including appraisals by clients; a board of directors who oversees such an evaluation and who carries on some part of it independent of staff; processes which insure that boards of directors can in fact carry out their accountability functions; evaluation procedures which not only go from the top down but also from the bottom up; and ongoing staff-board dialogues.

Such a step by NASW would do more toward improving the practice of social agencies than any other single act. It would establish consequences for poor practice in agencies which all too often exist in a land of no consequences. But, such a system would immediately bring NASW into conflict with some of its key members who are directors of large agencies. For an association to put on probation or rescind the credentials of an agency on whom, to a certain extent, its survival depends is admittedly a difficult task.

Credentialling bodies have a long history of coming under the control of those they are designed to control (Goodman, 1964),

Pressure is brought to appoint the right people to such commissions, people who play ball. Commissioners also fear that the wrong people will suffer if an organization is censured. If workers will not work for particular social agencies, the clients may suffer.

There is status difference between the directors of large and prestigious agencies and the staff members of credentialling bodies. The lowly tend not to antagonize the mighty, for some day they might need their assistance. Ultimately, large agencies are treated gingerly, small agencies are roasted. This disparity of treatment eventually corrodes the work of the regulatory body.

Nevertheless, the battle to get NASW and other professional associations to shift their priorities must be waged. An agency's desire for prestige can be utilized to influence that agency to improve its practice. If M.S.W.s will not work for particular agencies, these agencies might seek other sources of personnel. More likely, they would try to keep their problems from becoming public knowledge and seek some accommodation.

Leadership

Changing structures and procedures of organizations can often mitigate strains and dilemmas. In the long run, however, an organization needs an ongoing mechanism to cope with new and emerging tensions. Leadership provides such a mechanism. Insuring that agencies have the leadership to perform such a function is the second long-range aim of the staff. In the Met City Welfare Department, Bill Johnson sought changes that would allow effective leadership to develop. He didn't simply seek to have the director fired.

Acknowledging the value of leadership does not mean rejecting the idea that staff should participate in agency decision-making. It does mean rejecting the idea that simply by decentralizing, expanding job responsibilities, and developing authentic interpersonal relationships, autonomous self-directing workers will emerge, able to resolve organizational problems and strains in a quasi-legislative fashion.

Leadership will still be required. First, the planning and management of an organization requires specific expertise. Second, there is an ongoing need to reconcile the dilemmas and strains of organizational life. Third and most importantly, as long as there is concern for effectiveness in an organization, there will be considerable strain between the needs of individuals for self-actualization and the needs of organizations for achievement and efficiency.

People bring different personalities and habits to their work. Some are extremely passive, some seek to gain authority, some seek recognition, and some have strong needs for security. These personal needs, attitudes, and prejudices are not easily molded into cooperative efforts. Doing away with authority relationships does not necessarily change people. Even in nondirective therapeutic relationships, change does not necessarily result.

Most organizations have a variety of goals as well as an overriding desire to maintain their stability and survival. They are seldom able to optimize, but must satisfy or do the best they can under the constraints they must live with. An organization is "a mechanism which buffers and balances between external and internal pressures, a structure which [satisfies] between conflicting requirements rather than a structure which maximizes any one of them separately" (Adizes, 1971, pp. 233–234).

Judgment and disagreement must eventually come into play. Leadership is necessary to coordinate the parts of an organization when agreement cannot be secured (Thompson, 1967, pp. 133–141). Fluctuations in motivation, limitations of ability, breakdowns in communication, personal conflicts, and failures in coordination make leadership essential.

Leadership can function in many ways. McDonald's leadership style was considerably different from that of the traditional bureaucratic structure. Here, staff delegates authority to the organization's leadership as much as receives it from them. Authority is legitimated not so much by virtue of office as by competence; it is maintained not so much by rewards and punishments as by common commitment to objectives.

Leadership should proceed by consultation with staff. Authority is not maintained to decide for others, but to insure organizational adaptability in the face of strains and conflicts which otherwise could not be bridged. Kahn and Boulding (1964, p. 4) make the point: "The argument for the essentiality of power to an organization is not an argument for authoritarianism. To say that an organization must be able to attain a certain level of power over the activities of its members is not to specify the bases and sources of that power. The basis may be punishment or identification with the organizational goal; the source may be a formal leader or the entire peer group. . . . It is essential that an organization be able to exert power over the behavior of its members; it is not essential that such power be concentrated in a few hands or enforced by threats or penalties."

Whatever innovations staff pursue, it is incumbent on them to recognize the vital role leadership must play. How much decentralization, how much expansion in job responsibility, and how much participative management can only be determined through experimentation in particular situations. While all tasks are not the same in their need for expertise and control, evidence indicates that a good deal of flattening of the hierarchical pyramid should be attempted (Lee and Shepard, 1971). Excessive hierarchy, specialization, and centralization tend to subvert the best of accountability systems (Wilensky, 1967). Yet, there is little evidence to suggest that agencies are best run as legislatures. Voting and other forms of political decision-making are not easily transferable to the work situation (Adizes, 1971, pp. 247–251).

Strategy and Tactics

The achievement of such long-range aims by staff as securing effective leadership and accountability systems is important. Yet there are often problems which, though related to these larger ends, nevertheless demand immediate attention. Strategy and tactics as well as timing are crucial to their attainment.

While the connection between long- and short-range targets of change may not initially be clear, it is possible to approach problems in a systematic manner. First, one must be absolutely clear about what one wishes to change and about the problems that can be anticipated in initiating and implementing the solution. While this is an obvious rational approach, it is quite a complicated task.

There are a variety of potential approaches to any particular problem, such as getting a traditional casework agency to institute family therapy. One might attempt to restructure a board so that tensions developed through agency evaluations would result in an innovative spirit in the agency.

One might take the more immediate approach of stalking the lion by arranging for a series of speakers on family therapy, quietly doing some family therapy, documenting results, building alliances among key staff members, and thereby manipulating the director toward the desired end. One might even decide that getting the director fired is the most appropriate tack.

Knowing one's options is important, yet before an option is chosen a number of steps must be taken. Maria Hanrahan went through the following process before deciding not to seek the removal of Ms. Bowden. First, determine the factors inside and outside the organization that affect the problem. Jenkins (1964) provides a useful model for making such an analysis.

Second, determine where in the organization the decision to change can be made. Determine who has the formal authority to make the decision and who or which groups can influence the decision.

Third, anticipate the amount of resistance to the proposed solution. Determine whether those who have authority and influence agree on the issue and how they will resolve any disagreement. Find out if they are unaware that a problem really exists or are diametrically opposed because of a clash of interests and values. Past experiences in the agency around similar issues and discussions with other staff can provide some of the answers.

Finally, timing is crucial. Nonprofit organizations are generally more amenable to change in program when their budgets are expanding or declining, when other agencies begin competing for their clients, when their performance reports are questioned, when their clientele change, or when new technologies are widely hailed.

Going through the above analytic steps, in planning a changeover to family therapy for example, can help a social worker decide whether there is a chance of success in the short run and whether the anticipated result is worth the effort required. Few changes will come easily.

The worker must next develop strategy and tactics related to a course of action. When there is issue dissensus and difference, as in most of the cases presented, an adversary or pressure type of strategy will be required. Influence must be based on factors other than simply the ability to rationally persuade. Procedures must be used other than those formally prescribed by the agency.

Patti and Resnick (1972, p. 56) make the point that "agency workers usually think of change activities as occurring in formal contexts both internal and external to the organization. [They] present their plan of action to decision-makers through memos, letters, special meetings and conferences, or the development of formal relationships . . . [with] professional associations, educational institutions, and the like. As a result, the plan of action surfaces prematurely, and the change effort languishes for lack of support."

All of the cases presented illustrate a much broader range of action open to workers. These include: formality-informality, overtness-covertness, and internality-externality. Clearly, formality and explicitness are quite limiting.

Formal and Overt. A great deal of influence can be garnered by developing a reputation for personal competence or for having political contacts or by making what's happening in an agency highly visible. However, the resistance to tensions that will develop in most cases make it unlikely that overt tactics alone can carry the day. Resistance must be overcome.

Formal and Covert. Stalking the lion, developing an organizational tool such as Concerned MSWs, and organizing parents of club members to help with program are examples of formal activities whose real ends are hidden. They are designed to keep the usual ways in which changes are blocked from coming into play or at least to delay their impact.

Informal and Overt. More can often be accomplished informally than formally because of the risks involved in formal confrontation. A variety of potential allies, both internal and external to the organization, must be contacted informally to determine the extent of their support and commitment.

Informal and Covert. Liberation or an exposé cannot be effective if the source is immediately visible. Change entails risks. Tension is uncomfortable. Most people are not willing to take real risks if there is no possibility of escape in case of failure. Potential rewards are always discounted by potential costs.

In developing their tactics, staff are able to take advantage of the fact that influence is not static (Mechanic, 1962). It increases and decreases depending on its source. Unrelated actions, whose purpose is to develop a base of influence from which can be pyramided other sources of influence, can be carried out. One's ability to influence because of one's competence can be pyramided into influence based on the ability to articulate values to which others are drawn. This ultimately can be pyramided into the ability to reward and punish. Witness Ms. Berglinder's struggle with the chief of the TB ward at Maimonides.

In pyramiding their influence, staff have an impressive array of tools including citizen groups, unions, professional organizations, ombudsmen, politicians, media, staff organizations, clients, and the courts. Staff can, if they choose an adversary strategy, engage in litigation, picket, make previously hidden conditions visible, bargain, build alliances, contrive crises, bring sanctions to bear through external interest groups, encourage noncompliance with agency policy, and engage in fait accomplis (Specht, 1969, pp. 10–11).

> *Should they choose a more collaborative strategy they can . . . provide information about the nature of the problem, (2) present alternative courses of action (programs, procedures, and the like), (3) request support for experimentation. . . . (4) Seek to establish a committee to study and make recommendations on alternative approaches to a problem, (5) create new opportunities for interaction . . . to express ideas and feelings, build trust, and learn better ways to communicate. . . . (6) Make appeals to conscience, professional ethics, and values, and (7) persuade by logical argument . . . and (8) point out the negative consequences of continuing a specific policy [Patti and Resnick, 1972, p. 54].*

While the focus in most of the cases discussed has been strategy and tactics of overcoming resistances to change, the process through which change takes place must be understood. The initiation of change often requires a different approach than the implementation. Yet often it may not be clear, even after extensive analysis of a problem, just what should be done. At certain points one may have to switch from an adversary approach to a collaborative one and vice versa. Mistakes will occur. Alterations and adjustments in plans will have to be made.

Oftentimes such changes are required because of the values and personality of those involved. For example, a major stumbling block to innovation in social agencies can be a clash in values over such issues as the relative utility of punishment as opposed to love, or the advisability of offering help as opposed to the desirability of struggle and self-reliance. These are difficult issues to resolve.

Educational or consciousness-raising processes alone seldom have much utility, especially in the short run. A more promising approach is to raise countervailing values which mute the conflict, as Amy Abramson did when she was arguing from the basis of a smooth functioning ward rather than good patient care. Thus she was able to secure time to meet with the doctors, involve them in her work with the patients, and thereby allow for the possibility of the development of new and different values on their part.

Sensitivity to peer pressure is extremely important in dealing with value conflicts. Most individuals take their cues from the leaders of such reference groups. Countless, programmatic innovations have foundered on the shoals of client, inmate, guard, supervisor, or doctor resistance. This resistance, while often rooted in values, is similarly rooted in emotions. This emotional element is related to wanting to feel in control of one's life and work. Carol Whitebone understood that the therapeutic team would never work if the attendants weren't given assistance when their work became overwhelming. If the emotional element is considered, often the value issue is more amenable to change.

Those who plan change must also recognize the psychological problems that change induces. It is difficult to work in a state of uncertainty, admit error, open one's values and commitments to reevaluation, and be confused about one's role. Being the proponent of change somewhat mitigates these problems.

Nevertheless, as noted in several of the cases, maintaining the commitment of one's allies over long periods of time is a serious dilemma. People leave, get promoted, develop other interests, drop out because of fear of reprisal, or are uncomfortable about violating organizational norms. The options open for inducing change are often severely constrained by the need to maintain one's support. If picketing is anathema to a great number of staff, such a tactic is used with considerable peril to one's overall goals.

The tactics one can use will also be constrained by the personalities of one's opponents. A particular strategy will succeed in one situation and fail in another simply because of the personalities involved. Change generally produces anxiety. Understanding the ordinary defense mechanisms and how to manage them can be of great help in mapping tactics and strategies. Administrators who need to control can often make startling organizational innovations if they think the innovation is their own.

There is a personal side to planning organizational change. The reformer tends to involve himself passionately in his causes. This moral investment has a number of traps: defining the opposition as morally inferior, blindness to one's own selfish ego involvement, inability to see how one's motives could be questioned by others, lack of appreciation of the interests and concerns of those who resist change, and the inability to question whether in fact one's reforms will work. Humility, intelligence, and self-awareness are required.

The Professional Employee

It is impossible to write about changing social agencies without considering their radical critics. What is the value of making a foster care agency more effective when the conditions which cause family breakup are endemic in the structure of society? Should not these resources and efforts be geared toward changing these conditions rather than maintaining at best an ameliorative structure? Do not social workers who operate in prisons where brutality exists merely maintain such a system by their feeble efforts at helping one or two prisoners? These are serious charges.

The poverty program is a case in point. Local community boards were created to administer poverty funds which were inadequate to deal with the problems related to poverty. Ultimately, factions took to fighting each other for control of the boards rather than coalescing to fight for adequate financing. The inadequacy of the funds was overlooked. This same sham can occur on boards of social agencies: people fighting each other to improve agency practices when the agency operating at its peak cannot even make a dent in the social problem it is supposedly addressing.

The answers to such charges must, of necessity, be individual. Some agencies should not be maintained. The public should not be allowed to have the illusion that an agency is doing anything really worthwhile when it is not. There is a place for moral outrage. Some battles have to be fought even though they cannot be won.

Yet, those who claim that it is useless to help people when the social causes of their problems still exist are generally those who do not need help. A great many people cannot afford to wait for help.

The strongest argument for maintaining a focus on results, especially a focus on what clients say about an agency (Mayer and Timms, 1970), is that such a focus would tend to insure the visibility of just what social agencies can and cannot contribute to the solution of social problems. All too often social agencies become the buffers between social problems and the public, with a consequent loss of public understanding and support for change. The more everyone knows about what social agencies do, the better off agencies and their clients will be.

One final word remains to be said about the influence of lower level staff. Some may feel that staff influence will result in organizational warfare and anarchy—a constant round of attack and retaliation. There are several checks on this eventuality.

Most professional staff are not irresponsible. Those who are will not be made more irresponsible by the reading of this book. They are already acting irresponsibly. Subversion for personal or ideological ends not sanctioned by a board must be stopped. Leadership has the authority to stop it.

Locating ultimate accountability at the board level and insisting that the board have independent access to information about agency functioning not only puts limits on the administration, it also severely constrains manipulative staff. They will have great difficulty manipulating all the facts.

Most importantly, in an agency geared to consultative management, the spirit will insure the majority will not condone the subversive tendencies of a few. Rather, staff will work to maintain a context in which both administration and staff are held to account for results achieved. This is the only legitimate end of staff moving out of channels and crossing the Rubicon of influence.

Bibliography

ADIZES, I. *Industrial Democracy: Yugoslav Style.* New York: Free Press, 1971.

ALINSKY, S. *Rules for Radicals.* New York: Random House, 1971.

ARGYRIS, C. "Excerpts from the Impact of Budgets on People." In H. Schatz (Ed.), *Social Work Administration: A Resource Book.* New York: Council on Social Work Education, 1970.

BANFIELD, E. *Political Influence.* New York: Free Press, 1961.

BECK, B. "Mobilization for Youth: Reflections About Its Administration." In H. H. Weissman (Ed.), *Justice and the Law in the Mobilization for Youth Experience.* New York: Association Press, 1969.

BERLINER, A. K. "Some Pitfalls in Administrative Behavior." *Social Casework,* 1971, *52,* 562–566.

BIRNBAUM, M. "Sense About Sensitivity Training." *Saturday Review,* Nov. 15, 1969, 82–83, 96–98.

BLAU, P. *The Dynamics of Bureaucracy.* Chicago: University of Chicago Press, 1955.

BRAGER, G. "Effecting Organizational Change Through a Demonstration Project: The Case of the Schools." In G. Brager and F. Purcell (Eds.), *Community Action Against Poverty.* New Haven: College and University Press, 1967.

139

CLARK, B. "Organizational Adaptation and Precarious Values." In A. Etzioni (Ed.), *Complex Organizations.* New York: Holt, Rinehart, and Winston, 1961.

CYERT, R. M., and MARCH, J. G. "The Behavioral Theory of the Firm: A Behavioral Science-Economics Amalgam." In W. W. Cooper, H. J. Leavitt, and M. W. Shelley (Eds.), *New Perspectives in Organizational Behavior.* New York: John Wiley, 1964.

DOWNS, A. *Inside Bureaucracy.* Boston: Little, Brown and Company, 1967.

DUMONT, M. "Down the Bureaucracy." *Transaction,* 1970, *7,* 10–14.

EATON, J. W. "Symbolic and Substantive Evaluative Research." *Administrative Science Quarterly,* 1962, *6,* 421–442.

ENELOW, J. A., and WESTON, W. D. "Cooperation or Chaos: The Mental Health Administrator's Dilemma." Unpublished paper delivered at the American Orthopsychiatric Association Convention, Washington, D.C., Mar. 1971.

ETZIONI, A. "Two Approaches to Organizational Analysis: A Critique and a Suggestion." *Administrative Science Quarterly,* 1960, *5,* 257–278.

GEORGOPOULOS, G. "An Open-System Theory Model for Organizational Research." In A. Negandhi and J. Schnitter (Eds.), *Organizational Behavior Models.* Kent, Ohio: Kent State University, 1970.

GOLDBERG, J. R. "The Professional and His Union in the Jewish Center." *Journal of Jewish Communal Service,* 1960, *36,* 284–289.

GOODMAN, W. *All Honorable Men.* London: Longmans, Green, and Company, 1964.

GOULDNER, A. *Patterns of Industrial Democracy.* New York: Free Press, 1954.

GROSS, N., GIACQUINTA, J., and BERNSTEIN, M. *Implementing Organizational Innovations.* New York: Basic Books, 1971.

JAY, A. *Management and Machiavelli.* New York: Bantam, 1969.

JENKINS, D. H. "Force Field Analysis Applied to a School Situation." In W. Bennis, K. Benne, and R. Chin (Eds.), *The Planning of Change.* New York: Holt, Rinehart, and Winston, 1964.

KADUSHIN, A. "Child Welfare." In H. Mass (Ed.), *Research in the Social Services.* New York: National Association of Social Workers, 1971.

KAHN, R., and BOULDING, E. (Eds.). *Power and Conflict in Organizations.* New York: Basic Books, 1964.

LEE, J. C., and SHEPARD, J. M. "Participative Management and Voluntary Turnover: Concepts, Theories, and Implications for Management." In *Working Papers No. 1, National Study of Social Welfare and Rehabilitation Workers*. Washington, D.C.: Department of Health, Education, and Welfare, 1971.

LINDSEY, P. C. "Points and Viewpoints; Strategies in Perspective." *Social Work*, 1973, *18*, 109, 111–112.

LIPTON, H., and MALTER, S. "The Social Worker as Mediator on a Hospital Ward." In W. Schwartz and S. Zalba (Eds.), *The Practice of Group Work*. New York: Columbia University Press, 1971.

MAYER, J., and TIMMS, N. *The Client Speaks*. New York: Atherton, 1970.

MC CLEERY, R. H. "Policy Change in Prison Management." In A. Etzioni (Ed.), *Complex Organizations*. New York: Holt, Rinehart, and Winston, 1961.

MC GREGOR, D. *The Human Side of Enterprize*. New York: McGraw-Hill, 1960.

MECHANIC, D. "Sources of Power of Lower Participants in Complex Organizations." *Administrative Science Quarterly*, 1962, *3*, 349–364.

NADER, R., PETKAS, P., and BLACKWELL, K. *Whistle Blowing*. New York: Grossman, 1972.

PATTI, R., and RESNICK, H. "Changing the Agency from Within." *Social Work*, 1972, *17*, 48–57.

PERLMUTTER, E. "Decentralization of Schools Fails." *New York Times*, May 8, 1972, 1, 26.

PERROW, C. *Organizational Analysis*. Belmont, Calif.: Wadsworth, 1970.

PIVEN, H., and PAPPENFORT, D. "Strain Between Administrator and Worker: A View from the Field of Corrections." *Social Work*, 1960, *5*, 37–45.

REID, P. N. "Reforming the Social Services Monopoly." *Social Work*, 1972, *17*, 44–54.

REID, W. "Interagency Coordination in Delinquency Prevention and Control." *Social Service Review*, 1964, *38*, 418–428.

RIVLIN, A. *Systematic Thinking for Social Action*. Washington, D.C.: Brookings Institution, 1971.

ROSENBLATT, A. "Organizational Problems in Conducting Research: Social Research as a Social Process." *Social Work* (British) 1968, *25*, 9–16.

ROSSI, J. J., and FILSTEAD, W. J. *The Therapeutic Community*. New York: Behavioral Publications, 1972.

SCHERZ, F. H. "A Concept of Supervision Based on Definition of Job Responsibility." In *Proceedings, National Conference on Social Welfare*. New York: Columbia University Press, 1958.

SCHWARTZ, A. "PPBS and Evaluation and Research: Problems and Promises." In E. Schwartz (Ed.), *Planning Programming Budgeting Systems and Social Welfare*. Chicago: University of Chicago School of Social Service Administration, 1970.

SCOTT, W. R. "Professional Employees in a Bureaucratic Structure: Social Work." In A. Etzioni (Ed.), *The Semi-Professions and Their Organizations*. New York: Free Press, 1969.

SELZNICK, P. *The Organizational Weapon*. New York: McGraw-Hill, 1952.

SPECHT, H. "Disruptive Tactics." *Social Work*, 1969, *14*, 5–15.

STEIN, H. A. "Board, Executive and Staff." In *Proceedings, National Conference on Social Welfare, 1962*. New York: Columbia University Press, 1962.

SUCHMAN, E. A. *Evaluative Research*. New York: Russell Sage Foundation, 1967.

TAEBEL, D. "Strategies to Make Bureaucrats Responsive." *Social Work*, 1972, *17*, 38–43.

THOMPSON, J. D. *Organizations in Action*. New York: McGraw-Hill, 1967.

WADSWORTH, H. G. "Initiating a Preventive Corrective Approach in an Elementary School System." *Social Work*, 1970, *15*, 60–66.

WALKER, R. "The Ninth Panacea: Program Evaluation." *Evaluation*, 1972, *1*, 45–53.

WASSERMAN, H. "Early Careers of Professional Social Workers in a Public Child Welfare Agency." *Social Work*, 1970, *15*, 93–101.

WAX, J. "Developing Social Work Power in a Medical Organization." *Social Work*, 1968, *13*, 62–71.

WAX, J. "The Pros and Cons of Group Supervisions." *Social Casework*, 1959, *40*, 307–313.

WEISSMAN, H. H. *Community Councils and Community Control*. Pittsburgh: University of Pittsburgh Press, 1970.

WEISSMAN, H. H. "The Middle Road to Distributive Justice." *Social Work*, 1972, *17*, 86–93.

WERTZ, O. "Social Workers and the Therapeutic Community." *Social Work*, 1966, *11*, 43–49.

WILCOX, H. "Hierarchy, Human Nature and the Participative Panacea." *Public Administration Review*, 1969, *29*, 53–64.

WILENSKY, H. *Organizational Intelligence*. New York: Basic Books, 1967.

Index